THE

CONSTITUTION

OF THE

State of Maryland,

REPORTED AND ADOPTED BY THE CONVENTION OF DELEGATES ASSEMBLED AT THE CITY OF ANNAPOLIS, NOVEMBER 4th, 1850, AND SUBMITTED TO AND RATIFIED BY THE PEOPLE ON THE FIRST WEDNESDAY OF JUNE, 1851,

WITH

MARGINAL NOTES AND REFERENCES

To Acts of the General Assembly and Decisions of the Court of Appeals,

AND AN APPENDIX AND INDEX,

By EDWARD OTIS HINKLEY, Esq., *of the Baltimore Bar.*

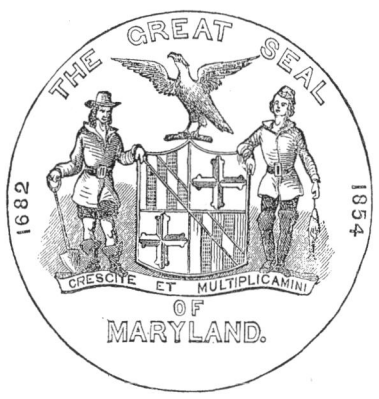

BALTIMORE:
PRINTED AND PUBLISHED BY JOHN MURPHY & CO.
No. 178 *Market Street.*
1855.

ENTERED, according to the Act of Congress, in the year 1855,
BY JOHN MURPHY & CO.
in the Clerk's Office of the District Court of Maryland.

ADVERTISEMENT.

THE publishers, in issuing this edition of the new Constitution, being desirous of making it as useful and acceptable to the public as possible, have procured the services of a gentleman of the Baltimore Bar, who has some experience in work of this kind, to make marginal notes, with references to the Acts of Assembly and Decisions of the Court of Appeals relating to it, and an Appendix containing some *notes* of the principal *changes* made in the old Constitution by this new one, with *remarks* upon their supposed *causes*, and references to the different articles, sections and clauses of the instrument which impose special duties upon the Legislature and upon officers of other departments; to which is added a very full Index.

It is believed that these additions will render this edition as complete as possible.

November, 1855.

Maryland State Convention.

CHAMBER OF HOUSE OF DELEGATES,
November 5th, 1850.

AT the hour of $12\frac{1}{2}$, on motion of Ex-Gov. SPRIGG, of Prince George's, the Convention was called to order, by inviting the Hon. BENJAMIN C. HOWARD, of Baltimore county, to the Chair.

On motion of Hon. ELIAS BROWN, of Carroll, JAMES L. RIDGELY, Esq., of Baltimore county, was appointed Secretary pro tem.

On motion of the Hon. WM. H. TUCK, of Prince George's, the Chair was authorized to appoint a committee of three, to wait on the Executive and obtain a list of the Delegates chosen to this Convention.

The Chair named Messrs. TUCK, of Prince George's, GWINN, of Baltimore city, and RICAUD, of Kent, as the committee.

Mr. TUCK, from the committee, appointed to wait on the Governor, to obtain a list of the Delegates elect to the Convention, reported that the committee had performed that duty, and that the Secretary of State was now in attendance with a communication from the Governor, touching that subject.

Whereupon, JOHN NICK WATKINS, Esq., Secretary of State, presented the following communication from the Governor to the Convention, together with the official returns of the election:

STATE DEPARTMENT, ANNAPOLIS, MD.
November 5th, 1850.

Gentlemen of the Convention:

I have the honor, in compliance with your request, to transmit herewith the returns of the election held on the first Wednesday of September last, under the Act of December Session, eighteen hundred and forty-nine, chapter three hundred and forty-six, entitled " an Act to provide for the taking of the sense of the people upon the expediency of calling a Convention to frame a new Constitution and form of Government for the State, and to provide for the election of Delegates to such Convention," and a list of the Delegates to the Convention.

PHILIP F. THOMAS.

A LIST OF
Members of the Maryland State Convention,

Elected under the provisions of the Act of the General Assembly of December Session 1849, ch. 346.

St. Mary's County.
GEORGE C. MORGAN,
WILLIAM J. BLACKISTONE,
JOHN F. DENT,
J. R. HOPEWELL.

Kent County.
JAMES B. RICAUD,
JOHN LEE,
EZEKIEL F. CHAMBERS,
JOSEPH T. MITCHELL.

Anne Arundel County.
THOMAS DONALDSON,
THOMAS B. DORSEY,
GEORGE WELLS,
ALEXANDER RANDALL,
JAMES KENT,
JOHN S. SELLMAN.

Calvert County.
GEORGE W. WEEMS,
J. J. DALRYMPLE,
JOHN BOND,
A. R. SOLLERS.

Baltimore County.
BENJAMIN C. HOWARD,
JAMES M. BUCHANAN,
EPHRAIM BELL,
THOMAS J. WELSH,
H. J. CHANDLER,
JAMES L. RIDGELY.

Charles County.
GEORGE BRENT,
JOHN G. CHAPMAN,
WILLIAM D. MERRICK,
DANIEL JENIFER.

Talbot County.
EDWARD LLOYD,
S. P. DICKINSON,
C. SHERWOOD,
M. O. COLSTON.

Somerset County.
JOHN DENNIS,
JAMES U. DENNIS,
J. W. CRISFIELD,
J. J. DASHIELL,
WILLIAM WILLIAMS.

Dorchester County.
THOMAS H. HICKS,
JOHN H. HODSON,
WM. T. GOLDSBOROUGH,
J. R. ECCLESTON,
FRANCIS P. PHELPS.

Cecil County.
ALBERT CONSTABLE,
B. B. CHAMBERS,
WILLIAM McCULLOUGH,
JOHN M. MILLER,
LOUIS McLANE.

MEMBERS OF THE CONVENTION.

Prince George's County.
THOMAS F. BOWIE,
WILLIAM H. TUCK,
SAMUEL SPRIGG,
JOHN M. S. McCUBBIN,
J. D. BOWLING.

Frederick County.
FRANCIS THOMAS,
EDWARD SHRIVER,
WILLIAM COST JOHNSON,
JOHN D. GAITHER,
DANIEL S. BISER,
ROBERT ANNAN.

Washington County.
GEORGE SCHLEY,
LEWIS P. FIERY,
ALEXANDER NEILL, Jr.,
JOHN NEWCOMER,
THOMAS HARBINE,
MICHAEL NEWCOMER.

Montgomery County.
J. M. KILGOUR,
ALLEN BOWIE DAVIS,
WASHINGTON WATERS,
JOHN BREWER,
JAMES W. ANDERSON.

Baltimore City.
CHARLES J. M. GWINN,
DAVID STEWART,
ROBERT J. BRENT,
GEORGE W. SHERWOOD,
BENJAMIN C. PRESSTMAN,
ELIAS WARE, Jr.

Worcester County.
L. L. DIRICKSON,
S. S. McMASTER,
E. HEARN,
JAMES M. FOOKS,
CURTIS W. JACOBS.

Harford County.
JOHN SAPPINGTON,
W. B. STEPHENSON,
R. McHENRY,
SAMUEL M. MAGRAW,
JAMES NELSON.

Alleghany County.
WILLIAM WEBER,
WILLIAM M. HOLLIDAY,
JOHN SLICER,
JAMES FITZPATRICK,
SAMUEL P. SMITH.

Queen Anne's County.
WILLIAM A. SPENCER,
WILLIAM GRASON,
ENOCH GEORGE,
HENRY E. WRIGHT.

Carroll County.
ANDREW G. EGE,
M. G. COCKEY,
JOSEPH M. PARKE,
JACOB SHOWER,
ELIAS BROWN.

Caroline County.
R. C. CARTER,
JOHN THAWLEY,
THOMAS R. STEWART,
EDWARD HARDCASTLE.

Officers of the Convention.

President..........Hon. JOHN G. CHAPMAN, of Charles Co.
Secretary..........GEORGE G. BREWER, of Annapolis.
Assistant Secretary..WASHINGTON B. CHICHESTER, of Montgomery Co.
Sergeant-at-Arms...RICHARD BOOTH, of Carroll Co.
Door-Keepers.......SAMUEL J. LAMBDIN and S. C. HERBERT.
Committee Clerks...J. W. RIDER,   GEO. S. KING,   J. MORRITZ,
              S. PEACOCK,   WILLIAM HALL.

Standing Committees.

Committee to consider and report a Declaration of Rights:
Messrs. Dorsey,   Biser,   Parke,   Wright.
        Williams,   Blackistone,   Hodson,

Committee to consider and report respecting the Executive Department:
Messrs. Grason,   Jenifer,   Goldsborough,   Holliday.
        Sprigg,   Bell,   Hearn,

Committee to consider and report respecting the Appointment, Tenure of Office, Duties and Compensation of all civil officers not embraced in the duties of other standing committees:
Messrs. Tuck,   Dent,   Jas. U. Dennis,   Lee.
        Brent, of Balt.   Weber,   McHenry,

Committee to consider and report respecting Treasury Department:
Messrs. McLane,   Nelson,   Bowling,   Dashiell.
        Donaldson,   Neill,   Sherwood, of Talbot,

Committee to consider and report respecting the Elective Franchise:
Messrs. Chambers,   Brown,   Weems,   John Newcomer,
        of Kent,   Hicks,   Thawley,   Slicer.

Committee on Accounts:
Messrs. Wells,   Williams,   Lloyd,   Neill,   Ware.

Committee to close the Accounts, &c., of the Convention after its Session:
Messrs. Randall,   Ware,   Magraw.

Committee to consider and report respecting the power of the Legislature on Corporations, Municipal and others, and on the power of the Legislature to create Debt:
Messrs. Wells,   Dirickson,   Waters,   Sherwood, of Balt.
        Ridgely,   Stewart, of Caroline,   Mitchell.

STANDING COMMITTEES.

Committee to consider and report respecting the Legislative Department:

Messrs. Johnson, Presstman, Kilgour, Carter. Phelps, Morgan, McCullough,

Committee to consider and report respecting Judiciary Department, embracing Common Law Courts, Courts of Equity, Orphans' Courts, Magistrates' Courts, and Justices of the Peace, and the mode of appointment and tenure of office:

Messrs. Bowie, Randall, Constable, Schley,
*Thomas, Stewart, Brent, Eccleston,
Chrisfield, of Balt., of Charles, Anderson.
Buchanan, Ricaud, Spencer,

Committee to consider and report respecting the office of Attorney-General and his Deputies:

Messrs. Shriver, Brewer, Miller, Colston.
Dalrymple, Fiery, Cockey,

Committee to consider and report respecting future amendments and revisions of the Constitution:

Messrs. Sollers, Jacobs, Gaither, Welsh.
Fitzpatrick, Sappington, Hardcastle,

Committee to consider and report a proper basis of Representation in the two Houses of the General Assembly, and a proper apportionment of representation in the same:

Messrs. Merrick, Chambers, of Kent, Lloyd, Harbine,
Howard, Gwinn, Ege, John Dennis, Kent.

Committee to consider and report respecting the Regulation of Inspections:

Messrs. Sellman, M. Newcomer, Ware, Chambers,
Hopewell, Fooks, Annan, of Cecil.

Committee to consider and report such provisions proper to be embodied in a Constitution for the State, as are not embraced in the foregoing resolutions:

Messrs. Jenifer, Dorsey, Blackistone, Johnson,
McLane, Brent, of Balt. Grason.

Committee of Revision:

Messrs. Tuck, Chambers, Grason, Randall, Magraw.
Afterwards added: Messrs. Donaldson, Gwinn.

Committee to consider and report respecting the Militia and Military Affairs:

Messrs. Howard, Shower, Dickinson, Schley.
Hearn, Bond, Stephenson,

Committee to consider and report respecting Education:

Messrs. Smith, Magraw, Chandler, George.
Davis, McCubbin, McMaster,

Committee on Printing:

Messrs. Stewart, Bowie, Johnson, Ricaud,
of Balt. Randall, Spencer, Weber.

* Mr. Thomas was excused at his own request from continuing a member of this Committee, and Mr. Morgan was appointed in his place.

Constitution of Maryland,

ADOPTED IN CONVENTION,

WHICH ASSEMBLED AT THE CITY OF ANNAPOLIS, ON THE FOURTH DAY OF NOVEMBER, EIGHTEEN HUNDRED AND FIFTY, AND ADJOURNED ON THE THIRTEENTH DAY OF MAY, EIGHTEEN HUNDRED AND FIFTY-ONE.

THE DECLARATION OF RIGHTS.

We, the People of the State of Maryland, grateful to Almighty God for our civil and religious liberty, and taking into our serious consideration the best means of establishing a good Constitution in this State, for the sure foundation and more permanent security thereof, declare:

ARTICLE 1. That all government of right originates from the people, is founded in compact only, and instituted solely for the good of the whole; and they have at all times, according to the mode prescribed in this Constitution, the unalienable right to alter, reform, or abolish their form of government, in such manner as they may deem expedient. *[Origin and Foundation of Government. Right of Reform.]*

ART. 2. That the people of this State ought to have the sole and exclusive right of regulating the internal government and police thereof. *[State's Rights.]*

ART. 3. That the inhabitants of Maryland are entitled to the common law of England, and the trial by jury according to the course *[Common Law. 2 Md. 429. Trial by Jury.]*

of that law, and to the benefit of such of the English statutes as existed on the fourth day of July, seventeen hundred and seventy-six, and which, by experience, have been found applicable to their local and other circumstances, and have been introduced, used and practised by the courts of law or equity, and also of all acts of Assembly in force on the first Monday of November, eighteen hundred and fifty, except such as may have since expired, or may be altered by this Constitution, subject, nevertheless, to the revision of, and amendment or repeal by the Legislature of this State; and the inhabitants of Maryland are also entitled to all property derived to them from or under the charter granted by his Majesty Charles the First, to Cæcilius Calvert, Baron of Baltimore.

English Statutes.
Acts of Assembly
Charter of the State.

ART. 4. That all persons invested with the Legislative or Executive powers of government, are the trustees of the public, and as such accountable for their conduct; wherefore, whenever the ends of government are perverted, and public liberty manifestly endangered, and all other means of redress are ineffectual, the people may, and of right ought to reform the old or establish a new government. The doctrine of non-resistance against arbitrary power and oppression is absurd, slavish and destructive of the good and happiness of mankind.

Right of Reform.

ART. 5. That the right of the people to participate in the Legislature is the best security of liberty, and the foundation of all free government; for this purpose elections ought to

Right of Suffrage.

DECLARATION OF RIGHTS. 11

be free and frequent, and every free white male citizen having the qualifications prescribed by the Constitution, ought to have the right of suffrage.

ART. 6. That the legislative, executive and judicial powers of government ought to be forever separate and distinct from each other; and no person exercising the functions of one of said departments, shall assume or discharge the duties of any other. *Separation of the Departments of Government.* *2 Md. 341.* *do. 429.*

ART. 7. That no power of suspending laws, or the execution of laws, unless by or derived from the Legislature, ought to be exercised or allowed. *Suspension of Laws.*

ART. 8. That freedom of speech and debate or proceedings in the Legislature, ought not to be impeached in any court of judicature. *Freedom of Speech.*

ART. 9. That Annapolis be the place for the meeting of the Legislature; and the Legislature ought not to be convened or held at any other place but from evident necessity. *Seat of Government.*

ART. 10. That for the redress of grievances, and for amending, strengthening and preserving the laws, the Legislature ought to be frequently convened. *Meeting of Legislature.*

ART. 11. That every man hath a right to petition the Legislature for the redress of grievances in a peaceable and orderly manner. *Right of Petition.*

ART. 12. That no aid, charge, tax, burthen, or fees, ought to be rated or levied, under any pretence, without the consent of the Legislature. *Levying of Taxes.*

ART. 13. That the levying of taxes by the poll is grievous and oppressive, and ought to be abolished; that paupers ought not to be assessed for the support of Government, but *Poll taxes oppressive.* *Paupers not to be taxed.*

every other person in the State, or person holding property therein, ought to contribute his proportion of public taxes, for the support of Government, according to his actual worth in real or personal property; yet fines, duties, or taxes may properly and justly be imposed or laid, on persons or property, with a political view, for the good government and benefit of the community.

Taxation according to actual worth. Fines, &c.

ART. 14. That sanguinary laws ought to be avoided as far as is consistent with the safety of the State; and no law to inflict cruel and unusual pains and penalties ought to be made in any case, or at any time hereafter.

Sanguinary Laws.

ART. 15. That retrospective laws, punishing acts committed before the existence of such laws, and by them only declared criminal, are oppressive, unjust and incompatible with liberty; wherefore, no ex post facto law ought to be made.

Retrospective Laws.

ART. 16. That no law to attaint particular persons of treason or felony, ought to be made in any case, or at any time hereafter.

Attainder.

ART. 17. That every free man, for any injury done to him in his person or property, ought to have remedy by the course of the law of the land, and ought to have justice and right, freely without sale, fully without any denial, and speedily without delay, according to the law of the land.

Right to have justice.

ART. 18. That the trial of facts where they arise, is one of the greatest securities of the lives, liberties, and estate of the people.

Trial of facts where they arise.

ART. 19. That in all criminal prosecutions, every man hath a right to be informed of the

Criminal Prosecutions.

DECLARATION OF RIGHTS. 13

accusation against him; to have a copy of the indictment or charge, in due time (if required) to prepare for his defence; to be allowed counsel; to be confronted with the witnesses against him; to have process for his witnesses; to examine the witnesses for and against him on oath; and to a speedy trial by an impartial jury, without whose unanimous consent he ought not to be found guilty.

ART. 20. That no man ought to be compelled to give evidence against himself in a court of common law, or in any other court, but in such cases as have been usually practised in this State, or may hereafter be directed by the Legislature. *Evidence against oneself.*

ART. 21. That no free man ought to be taken or imprisoned, or disseized of his freehold, liberties or privileges, or outlawed, or exiled, or in any manner destroyed, or deprived of his life, liberty or property, but by the judgment of his peers, or by the law of the land; provided, that nothing in this article shall be so construed as to prevent the Legislature from passing all such laws for the government, regulation and disposition of the free colored population of this State as they may deem necessary. *Freemen not to be imprisoned, &c., but by Law.* *2 Md. 429.* *Colored Population.*

ART. 22. That excessive bail ought not to be required, nor excessive fines imposed, nor cruel or unusual punishment inflicted by the courts of law. *Bail, Fines, &c.*

ART. 23. That all warrants, without oath, or affirmation, to search suspected places, or to seize any person or property, are grievous and oppressive; and all general warrants to search *Search Warrants.*

14 DECLARATION OF RIGHTS.

suspected places, or to apprehend suspected persons, without naming or describing the place, or the person in special, are illegal, and ought not to be granted.

Corruption of Blood, &c. ART. 24. That no conviction shall work corruption of blood, or forfeiture of estate.

Militia. ART. 25. That a well regulated militia is the proper and natural defence of a free government.

Standing Armies. ART. 26. That standing armies are dangerous to liberty, and ought not to be raised or kept up without the consent of the Legislature.

Military subject to Civil Power. ART. 27. That in all cases and at all times the military ought to be under strict subordination to, and control of, the civil power.

Quartering of Soldiers. ART. 28. That no soldier ought to be quartered in any house in time of peace without the consent of the owner, and in time of war in such manner only as the Legislature shall direct.

Martial Law. ART. 29. That no person, except regular soldiers, mariners, and marines, in the service of this State, or militia when in actual service, ought in any case be subject to, or punishable by, martial law.

Judges. ART. 30. That the independency and uprightness of Judges are essential to the impartial administration of justice, and a great security to the rights and liberties of the people; wherefore the Judges shall not be removed, except for misbehaviour, on conviction in a court of law, or by the Governor, upon the address of the General Assembly; *provided*, that two-thirds of all the members of each House concur in such address. No Judge

DECLARATION OF RIGHTS. 15

shall hold any other office, civil or military, or political trust or employment of any kind whatsoever, under the Constitution or Laws of this State, or of the United States, or any of them, or receive fees or perquisites of any kind for the discharge of his official duties. _{1 Md. 368.}

ART. 31. That a long continuance in the executive departments of power or trust is dangerous to liberty; a rotation, therefore, in those departments is one of the best securities of permanent freedom. _{Rotation in Offices.}

ART. 32. That no person ought to hold at the same time more than one office of profit, created by the Constitution or Laws of this State; nor ought any person in public trust to receive any present from any Foreign Prince, or State, or from the United States, or any of them, without the approbation of this State. _{Holding Offices. Presents.}

ART. 33. That as it is the duty of every man to worship God in such manner as he thinks most acceptable to Him, all persons are equally entitled to protection in their religious liberty, wherefore, no person ought, by any law, to be molested in his person or estate, on account of his religious persuasion or profession, or for his religious practice, unless under the color of religion any man shall disturb the good order, peace, or safety of the State, or shall infringe the laws of morality, or injure others in their natural, civil, or religious rights; nor ought any person to be compelled to frequent or maintain or contribute, unless on contract, to maintain any place of worship or any ministry; nor shall any person be deemed incompetent as a witness or juror who believes in the exist- _{Religious Liberty}

16 DECLARATION OF RIGHTS.

ence of a God, and that under his dispensation such person will be held morally accountable for his acts, and be rewarded or punished therefor, either in this world or the world to come.

Oaths of Office.

ART. 34. That no other test or qualification ought to be required, on admission to any office of trust or profit, than such oath of office as may be prescribed by this Constitution, or by the laws of the State, and a declaration of belief in the Christian religion; and if the party shall profess to be a Jew, the declaration shall be of his belief in a future state of rewards and punishments.

Disqualification of Ministers and Religious bodies from holding certain property.

3 Md. 119.

ART. 35. That every gift, sale or devise of land, to any minister, public teacher or preacher of the gospel, as such, or to any religious sect, order or denomination, or to or for the support, use or benefit of, or in trust for any minister, public teacher or preacher of the gospel as such, or any religious sect, order or denomination, and every gift or sale of goods or chattels to go in succession, or to take place after the death of the seller or donor, to or for such support, use or benefit; and, also, every devise of goods or chattels, to or for the support, use or benefit of any minister, public teacher or preacher of the gospel, as such; or any religious sect, order or denomination, without the leave of the Legislature, shall be void; except always, any sale, gift, lease or devise of any quantity of land, not exceeding five acres, for a church, meeting house or other house of worship, or parsonage, or for a burying ground, which shall be improved, en-

DECLARATION OF RIGHTS. 17

joyed or used only for such purpose; or such sale, gift, lease or devise shall be void.

ART. 36. That the manner of administering an oath or affirmation to any person, ought to be such as those of the religious persuasion, profession or denomination, of which he is a member, generally esteem the most effectual confirmation by the attestation of the Divine Being. *Administering of Oaths.*

ART. 37. That the city of Annapolis ought to have all its rights, privileges and benefits, agreeably to its charter, and the acts of Assembly confirming and regulating the same; subject to such alterations as have been or as may be made by the Legislature. *Rights of the City of Annapolis.*

ART. 38. That the liberty of the press ought to be inviolably preserved. *Liberty of the Press.*

ART. 39. That monopolies are odious, contrary to the spirit of a free government and the principles of commerce, and ought not to be suffered. *Monopolies.*

ART. 40. That no title of nobility or hereditary honors ought to be granted in this State. *Titles of Nobility, &c.*

ART. 41. That the Legislature ought to encourage the diffusion of knowledge and virtue, the promotion of literature, the arts, sciences, agriculture, commerce and manufactures, and the general melioration of the condition of the people. *Duties of the Legislature.*

ART. 42. This enumeration of rights shall not be construed to impair or deny others retained by the people. *Rights of the People.*

ART. 43. That this Constitution shall not be altered, changed, or abolished, except in the manner therein prescribed and directed. *Alteration of the Constitution.*

THE CONSTITUTION.

ARTICLE I.

ELECTIVE FRANCHISE.

Qualifications of voters.

SECTION 1. Every free white male person, of twenty-one years of age or upwards, who shall have been one year next preceding the election a resident of the State, and for six months a resident of the city of Baltimore, or of any county in which he may offer to vote, and being at the time of the election a citizen of the United States, shall be entitled to vote in the ward or election district in which he resides, *Vote by ballot.* in all elections hereafter to be held; and at all such elections the vote shall be taken by ballot. And in case any county or city shall be so divided as to form portions of different electoral districts for the election of Congressmen, Senator, delegate, or other officer or officers, then to entitle a person to vote for such officer, he must have been a resident of that *Division of counties, &c.* part of the county or city which shall form a part of the electoral district in which he offers to vote, for six months next preceding the election; but a person who shall have acquired a residence in such county or city entitling him to vote at any such election, shall be entitled to vote in the election district from which he *Change of Residence.* removed, until he shall have acquired a residence in the part of the county or city to which he has removed.

SEC. 2. That if any person shall give, or offer to give, directly or indirectly, any bribe, present or reward, or any promise, or any security for the payment or delivery of money or any other thing, to induce any voter to refrain from casting his vote, or forcibly to prevent him in any way from voting, or to obtain or procure a vote for any candidate or person proposed or voted for, as elector of President and Vice-President of the United States, or representative in Congress, or for any office of profit or trust created by the Constitution or laws of this State, or by the ordinances or authority of the Mayor and City Council of Baltimore, the person giving or offering to give, and the person receiving the same, and any person who gives or causes to be given an illegal vote, knowing it to be so, at any election to be hereafter held in this State, shall, on conviction in a court of law, in addition to the penalties now or hereafter to be imposed by law, be forever disqualified to hold any office of profit or trust, or to vote at any election thereafter. *Bribery.* *Penalties.*

SEC. 3. It shall be the duty of the General Assembly of Maryland to pass laws to punish with fine and imprisonment any person who shall remove into any election district or ward of the city of Baltimore, not for the purpose of acquiring a bona fide residence therein, but for the purpose of voting therein at an approaching election, or who shall vote in any election district or ward in which he does not *Laws against illegal voting.* *1853, ch. 133.*

reside, (except in the case provided for in the first article of the Constitution,) or shall, at the same election, vote in more than one election district or ward, or shall vote or offer to vote, in any name not his own, or in place of any other person of the same name, or shall vote in any county in which he does not reside.

Oath of Office.
1852, ch. 172.
1854, ch. 18.
4 Md. 189.

SEC. 4. Every person elected or appointed to any office of profit or trust under the Constitution or laws made pursuant thereto, before he shall enter upon the duties of such office shall take and subscribe the following oath or affirmation: I, A. B., do swear (or affirm, as the case may be,) that I will support the Constitution of the United States, and that I will be faithful and bear true allegiance to the State of Maryland, and support the Constitution and laws thereof; and that I will, to the best of my skill and judgment, diligently and faithfully, without partiality or prejudice, execute the office of ―――― according to the Constitution and laws of this State, and that since the adoption of the present Constitution, I have not, in any manner, violated the provisions thereof in relation to bribery of voters or preventing legal or procuring illegal votes to be given; (and if a Governor, Senator, member of the House of Delegates, or Judge,) "that I will not directly or indirectly receive the profits or any part of the profits of any other office during the time of my acting as ――――." And if any person elected or appointed to office as aforesaid, shall refuse or neglect to take the said oath or affirmation, he shall be considered as having refused to accept the said office, and a new election or appointment shall be made as in case of refusal or resignation, and any person swearing or affirming falsely in the premises, shall, on conviction thereof in a court of law, incur the penalties for wilful and corrupt perjury, and be thereafter incapable of voting at any election, and also incapable of holding any office of profit or trust in this State.

SEC. 5. That no person above the age of twenty-one years, convicted of larceny or other infamous crime, unless he shall be pardoned by the Executive, shall ever thereafter be entitled to vote at any election in this State, and no person under guardianship as a lunatic, or as a person non compos mentis, shall be entitled to vote. *Persons disqualified to vote.*

ARTICLE II.

EXECUTIVE DEPARTMENT.

SECTION 1. The Executive power of the State shall be vested in a Governor, whose term of office shall commence on the second Wednesday of January next ensuing his election, and continue for four years, and until his successor shall have qualified. *The Governor; his term of Office.*

SEC. 2. The first election for Governor under this Constitution shall be held on the first Wednesday in November, in the year eighteen hundred and fifty-three, and on the same day and month in every fourth year thereafter, at the places of voting for delegates to the General Assembly, and every person qualified to vote for delegates shall be qualified and entitled *Time, place, and manner of electing Governor.*

to vote for Governor; the election to be held in the same manner as the election of delegates, and the returns thereof, under seal, to be addressed to the Speaker of the House of Delegates, and enclosed and transmitted to the Secretary of State, and delivered to the said Speaker at the commencement of the session of the Legislature next ensuing said election.

SEC. 3. The Speaker of the House of Delegates shall then open the said returns, in the presence of both Houses, and the person having the highest number of votes, and being constitutionally eligible, shall be the Governor, and shall qualify in the manner herein prescribed, on the second Wednesday of January next ensuing his election, or as soon thereafter as may be practicable.

SEC. 4. If two or more persons shall have the highest and an equal number of votes, one of them shall be chosen Governor by the Senate and House of Delegates; and all questions in relation to the eligibility of Governor, and to the returns of said election, and to the number and legality of votes therein given, shall be determined by the House of Delegates. And if the person, or persons, having the highest number of votes be ineligible, the Governor shall be chosen by the Senate and House of Delegates. Every election of Governor, by the Legislature, shall be determined by a joint majority of the Senate and House of Delegates, and the vote shall be taken viva voce. But if two or more persons shall have the highest and an equal number of votes, then a second vote shall be taken, which shall be con-

STATE OF MARYLAND. 23

fined to the persons having an equal number; and if the votes should be again equal, then the election of Governor shall be determined by lot between those who shall have the highest and an equal number on the first vote.

SEC. 5. The State shall be divided into three districts; St. Mary's, Charles, Calvert, Prince George's, Anne Arundel, Montgomery, and Howard counties, and the city of Baltimore, to be the first; the eight counties of the Eastern Shore to be the second; and Baltimore, Harford, Frederick, Washington, Allegany and Carroll counties to be the third. The Governor, elected from the third district, in October last, shall continue in office during the term for which he was elected. The Governor shall be taken from the first district, at the first election of Governor under this Constitution; from the second district at the second election, and from the third district at the third election, and in like manner, afterwards, from each district in regular succession. *State divided into three Gubernatorial Districts, from which the Governor to be chosen in succession.*

SEC. 6. A person to be eligible to the office of Governor, must have attained the age of thirty years, and been for five years a citizen of the United States, and for five years next preceding his election a resident of the State, and for three years a resident of the district from which he was elected. *Qualification of Governor.*

SEC. 7. In case of the death or resignation of the Governor, or of his removal from the State, the General Assembly, if in session, or if not, at their next session, shall elect some other qualified resident of the same district, to *In case of death, &c., General Assembly to elect.*

be the Governor for the residue of the term for which the said Governor had been elected.

In case of vacancy during recess of Legislature—President of the Senate to act as Governor—or if he do not act, then the Speaker of the House of Delegates to act.

SEC. 8. In case of any vacancy in the office of Governor during the recess of the Legislature, the President of the Senate shall discharge the duties of said office till a Governor is elected as herein provided for; and in case of the death or resignation of said President, or of his removal from the State, or of his refusal to serve, then the duties of said office shall, in like manner, and for the same interval, devolve upon the Speaker of the House of Delegates, and the Legislature may provide by law for the case of impeachment or inability of the Governor, and declare what person shall perform the executive duties during such impeachment or inability; and for any vacancy in said office not herein provided for, provision may be made by law, and if such vacancy should occur without such provision being made, the Legislature shall be convened by the Secretary of State for the purpose of filling said vacancy.

Legislature to provide for Impeachment and for cases of vacancy not provided for.

Governor to be Commander-in-chief; but not to take the command in person.

SEC. 9. The Governor shall be commander-in-chief of the land and naval forces of the State, and may call out the militia to repel invasions, suppress insurrections, and enforce the execution of the laws; but shall not take the command in person without the consent of the Legislature.

His Duties.

SEC. 10. He shall take care that the laws be faithfully executed.

Appointment of Officers.

SEC. 11. He shall nominate, and by and with the advice and consent of the Senate, appoint all civil and military officers of the State, whose

STATE OF MARYLAND. 25

appointment or election is not otherwise herein provided for, unless a different mode of appointment be prescribed by the law creating the office.

SEC. 12. In case of any vacancy during the recess of the Senate in any office which the Governor has power to fill, he shall appoint some suitable person to said office, whose commission shall continue in force till the end of the next session of the Legislature, or till some other person is appointed to the same office, which ever shall first occur, and the nomination of the person thus appointed during the recess, or of some other person in his place, shall be made to the Senate, within thirty days after the next meeting of the Legislature. *Appointments during recess of Legislature.* *2 Md. 341.*

SEC. 13. No person, after being rejected by the Senate, shall be again nominated for the same office at the same session, unless at the request of the Senate; or be appointed to the same office during the recess of the Legislature. *Persons rejected not to be appointed.*

SEC. 14. All civil officers appointed by the Governor and Senate, shall be nominated to the Senate within fifty days from the commencement of each regular session of the Legislature; and their term of office shall commence on the first Monday of May next ensuing their appointment, and continue for two years (unless sooner removed from office) and until their successors respectively qualify according to law. *Time of Nomination.* *Term of Office.*

SEC. 15. The Governor may suspend or arrest any military officer of the State, for disobedience of orders, or other military offence, and may remove him in pursuance of the sen- *Courts-Martial.*

4

tence of a court-martial; and may remove, for incompetency or misconduct, all civil officers who receive appointments from the Executive for a term of years.

Extra Sessions of the Legislature.

SEC. 16. The Governor may convene the Legislature, or the Senate alone, on extraordinary occasions; and whenever, from the presence of an enemy or from any other cause, the seat of government shall become an unsafe place for the meeting of the Legislature, he may direct their sessions to be held at some other convenient place.

Governor to examine Treasury accounts.

SEC. 17. It shall be the duty of the Governor semi-annually, and oftener if he deem it expedient, to examine the bank-book, account books, and official proceedings of the Treasurer and Comptroller of the State.

Governor to recommend measures to Legislature.

SEC. 18. He shall from time to time inform the Legislature of the condition of the State, and recommend to their consideration such measures as he may judge necessary and expedient.

Pardoning Power

SEC. 19. He shall have power to grant reprieves and pardons, except in cases of impeachment, and in cases in which he is prohibited by other articles of this Constitution, and to remit fines and forfeitures for offences against the State; but shall not remit the principal or interest of any debt due to the State, except in cases of fines and forfeitures; and before granting a nolle prosequi, or pardon, he shall give notice in one or more newspapers, of the application made for it, and of the day on or after which his decision will be given; and in every case in which he exercises this

STATE OF MARYLAND. 27

power, he shall report to either branch of the Legislature, whenever required, the petitions, recommendations and reasons which influence his decision.

SEC. 20. The Governor shall reside at the seat of Government, and shall receive for his services an annual salary of thirty-six hundred dollars. <small>Governor's residence and salary.</small>

SEC. 21. When the public interest requires it, he shall have power to employ counsel, who shall be entitled to such compensation as the Legislature may allow in each case, after the services of such counsel shall have been performed. <small>May employ Counsel.</small>

SEC. 22. A Secretary of State shall be appointed by the Governor, by and with the advice and consent of the Senate, who shall continue in office, unless sooner removed by the Governor, till the end of the official term of the Governor from whom he received his appointment, and shall receive an annual salary of one thousand dollars. <small>Secretary of State. 1853, ch. 448.</small>

SEC. 23. He shall carefully keep and preserve a record of all official acts and proceedings, (which may, at all times, be inspected by a committee of either branch of the Legislature,) and shall perform such other duties as may be prescribed by law, or as may properly belong to his office. <small>His Duties.</small>

ARTICLE III.

LEGISLATIVE DEPARTMENT.

Two branches of the Legislature— Its style.

SECTION 1. The Legislature shall consist of two distinct branches, a Senate and a House of Delegates, which shall be styled "The General Assembly of Maryland."

Election of Senators.

SEC. 2. Every county of the State, and the city of Baltimore, shall be entitled to elect one Senator, who shall be elected by the qualified voters of the counties and city of Baltimore,

Their term of Office.

respectively, and who shall serve for four years from the day of their election.

Apportionment of Members of House of Delegates.

SEC. 3. The Legislature at its first session after the returns of the national census of eighteen hundred and sixty are published, and in like manner after each subsequent census, shall apportion the members of the House of Delegates among the several counties of the State, according to the population of each, and shall always allow to the city of Baltimore four more Delegates than are allowed to the most populous county, but no county shall be entitled to less than two members, nor shall the whole number of delegates ever exceed eighty, or be less than sixty-five; and until the apportionment is made under the census of eighteen hundred and sixty; St. Mary's county shall be entitled to two delegates; Kent, two; Anne Arundel, three; Calvert, two; Charles, two; Baltimore county, six; Talbot, two; Somerset, four; Dorchester, three; Cecil, three; Prince George's, three; Queen Anne's, two; Worcester, three; Frederick, six; Harford, three; Caroline, two; Baltimore city, ten; Washington, five; Montgomery, two; Allegany, four; Carroll, three, and Howard, two.

SEC. 4. The members of the House of Delegates shall be elected by the qualified voters of the counties and city of Baltimore respectively, to serve for two years from the day of their election. *Election of Delegates. Their term of Office.*

SEC. 5. The first election for delegates shall take place on the first Wednesday of November, eighteen hundred and fifty-one; and the elections for delegates and for one-half of the Senators, as nearly as practicable, shall be held on the same day in every second year thereafter, but an election for Senators shall be held in the year eighteen hundred and fifty-one, in Howard county, and all those counties in which senators were elected in the year eighteen hundred and forty-six. *Time of Elections.*

SEC. 6. Immediately after the Senate shall have convened after the first election under this Constitution, the Senators shall be divided, by lot, into two classes, as nearly equal in number as may be—the Senators of the first class shall go out of office at the expiration of two years, and Senators shall be elected on the first Wednesday of November, eighteen hundred and fifty-three, for the term of four years, to supply their places; so that, after the first election, one-half of the Senators may be chosen every second year; provided, that in no case shall any Senator be placed in a class which shall entitle him to serve for a longer term than that for which he was elected. In case the num- *Classification of Senators.*

30   CONSTITUTION OF THE

ber of Senators be hereafter increased, such classification of the additional Senators shall be made as to preserve as nearly as may be an equal number in each class.

Time of Meetings of the General Assembly. Their Sessions biennial

SEC. 7. The General Assembly shall meet on the first Wednesday of January, eighteen hundred and fifty two, on the same day, in the year eighteen hundred and fifty-three, and on the same day in the year eighteen hundred and fifty-four, and on the same day in every second year thereafter, and at no other time unless convened by the proclamation of the Governor.

Time of adjournment.

SEC. 8. The General Assembly may continue their first two sessions after the adoption of this Constitution, as long as, in the opinion of the two Houses, the public interests may require it, but all subsequent regular sessions of the General Assembly shall be closed on the tenth day of March next ensuing the time of their commencement, unless the same shall be closed at an earlier day by the agreement of the two Houses.

Qualifications of Senators and Delegates.

SEC. 9. No person shall be eligible as a Senator or Delegate who, at the time of his election, is not a citizen of the United States, and who has not resided at least three years next preceding the day of his election in this State, and the last year thereof in the county or city which he may be chosen to represent, if such county or city shall have been so long established, and if not, then in the county from which, in whole or in part, the same may have been formed; nor shall any person be eligible as a Senator unless he shall have attained the age of twenty-five years, nor as a delegate unless he shall have attained the age of twenty-one years at the time of his election.

SEC. 10. No member of Congress, or person holding any civil or military office under the United States, shall be eligible as a senator or delegate; and if any person shall, after his election as a Senator or Delegate, be elected to Congress, or be appointed to any office, civil or military, under the government of the United States, his acceptance thereof shall vacate his seat. Persons ineligible as Senators or Delegates.
1853, ch. 280.

SEC. 11. No Minister or Preacher of the Gospel, of any denomination, and no person holding any civil office of profit or trust under this State, except Justices of the Peace, shall be eligible as Senator or Delegate. Same.

SEC. 12. Each House shall be judge of the qualifications and elections of its members, subject to the laws of the State—appoint its own officers, determine the rules of its own proceedings, punish a member for disorderly or disrespectful behaviour, and with the consent of two-thirds, expel a member; but no member shall be expelled a second time for the same offence. Powers of each House.

SEC. 13. A majority of each House shall constitute a quorum for the transaction of business, but a smaller number may adjourn from day to day, and compel the attendance of absent members, in such manner and under such penalties as each House may prescribe. Quorum.

SEC. 14. The doors of each House and of committees of the whole shall be open, except when the business is such as ought to be kept secret. Sessions to be open.

32 CONSTITUTION OF THE

Journals to be published.

Yeas and Nays.
1853, ch. 36.

Special Adjournments.

Style of Laws.

Mode of their enactment.

Codification of Laws.
1852, Res. 4.

Amendments.

Additions.

SEC. 15. Each House shall keep a journal of its proceedings, and cause the same to be published. The yeas and nays of members on any question shall, at the call of any five of them, in the House of Delegates, or one in the Senate, be entered on the journal.

SEC. 16. Neither House shall, without the consent of the other, adjourn for more than three days; nor to any other place than that in which the House shall be sitting, without the concurrent vote of two-thirds of the members present.

SEC. 17. The style of all laws of this State shall be, "Be it enacted by the General Assembly of Maryland," and all laws shall be passed by original bill, and every law enacted by the Legislature shall embrace but one subject, and that shall be described in the title, and no law or section of law shall be revived, amended or repealed by reference to its title or section only; and it shall be the duty of the Legislature, at the first session after the adoption of this Constitution, to appoint two commissioners learned in the law, to revise and codify the laws of this State; and the said commissioners shall report the said code, so formed, to the Legislature, within a time to be by it determined, for its approval, amendment, or rejection; and if adopted, after the revision and codification of the said laws, it shall be the duty of the Legislature, in amending any article or section thereof, to enact the same as the said article or section would read when amended. And whenever the Legislature shall enact any public general law, not amendatory of any sec-

STATE OF MARYLAND. 33

tion or article in the said code, it shall be the duty of the Legislature to enact the same in articles and sections, in the same manner as the said code may be arranged; and to provide for the publication of all additions and alterations which may be made to the said code, and it shall also be the duty of the Legislature to appoint one or more commissioners learned in the law, whose duty it shall be to revise, simplify, and abridge the rules of practice, pleadings, forms of conveyancing, and proceedings of the Courts of record in this State. Rules of Practice, Pleading and Conveyancing to be revised. 1852, Res. 14.

SEC. 18. Any bill may originate in either House of the General Assembly, and be altered, amended or rejected by the other; but no bill shall originate in either House during the last three days of the session, or become a law, until it be read on three different days of the session in each House, unless three-fourths of the members of the House, where such bill is pending, shall so determine. Either House may originate Bills.

SEC. 19. No bill shall become a law unless it be passed in each House by a majority of the whole number of members elected, and on its final passage the ayes and noes be recorded. Passage of Bills.

SEC. 20. No money shall be drawn from the Treasury of the State, except in accordance with an appropriation made by law, and every such law shall distinctly specify the sum appropriated, and the object to which it shall be applied, provided that nothing herein contained shall prevent the Legislature from placing a contingent fund at the disposal of the Executive, who shall report to the Legislature at each session the amount expended and the Appropriations of money to be made by law. 4 Md. 189. Contingent fund.

purposes to which it was applied; an accurate statement of the receipts and expenditures of the public money shall be attached to and published with the laws after each regular session of the General Assembly.

SEC. 21. No divorce shall be granted by the General Assembly.

SEC. 22. No debt shall hereafter be contracted by the Legislature, unless such debt shall be authorized by a law providing for the collection of an annual tax or taxes sufficient to pay the interest on such debt as it falls due, and also to discharge the principal thereof within fifteen years from the time of contracting the same, and the taxes laid for this purpose shall not be repealed or applied to any other object until the said debt and the interest thereon shall be fully discharged, and the amount of debts so contracted and remaining unpaid shall never exceed one hundred thousand dollars. The credit of the State shall not, in any manner, be given or loaned to or in aid of any individual, association or corporation, nor shall the General Assembly have the power, in any mode, to involve the State in the construction of works of internal improvement, or in any enterprize which shall involve the faith or credit of the State, or make any appropriations therefor. And they shall not use or appropriate the proceeds of the internal improvement companies, or of the State Tax now levied, or which may hereafter be levied, to pay off the public debt, to any other purpose, until the interest and debt are fully paid, or the sinking fund shall be equal to the amount of the outstanding debt; but the Legislature may, without laying a tax, borrow an amount never to exceed fifty thousand dollars, to meet temporary deficiencies in the Treasury, and may contract debts to any amount that may be necessary for the defence of the State.

Temporary Deficiencies.

Defence of the State.

SEC. 23. No extra compensation shall be granted or allowed by the General Assembly to any public officer, agent, servant or contractor, after the services shall have been rendered or the contract entered into. Nor shall the salary or compensation of any public officer be increased or diminished during his term of office.

No extra Compensation or Increase of Salary to be allowed.

SEC. 24. No Senator or Delegate, after qualifying as such, shall, during the term for which he was elected, be eligible to any office which shall have been created, or the salary or profits of which shall have been increased during such term, or shall, during said term, hold any office or receive the salary or profits of any office, under the appointment of the Executive or Legislature.

Disqualification of Senators and Delegates to hold certain offices.

SEC. 25. Each House may punish by imprisonment, during the session of the General Assembly, any person not a member, for disrespectful or disorderly behaviour in its presence, or for obstructing any of its proceedings or any of its officers in the execution of their duties; *provided,* such imprisonment shall not, at any one time, exceed ten days.

Each House may imprison for disrespect.

SEC. 26. The members of each House shall, in all cases, except treason, felony, or other criminal offence, be privileged from arrest during their attendance at the session of the Gen-

Exemption from Arrest.

eral Assembly, and in going to and returning from the same, allowing one day for every thirty miles such member may reside from the place at which the General Assembly is convened.

No liability for words spoken in debate.

SEC. 27. No Senator or Delegate shall be liable, in any civil action or criminal prosecution whatever, for words spoken in debate.

Powers of the House of Delegates.

SEC. 28. The House of Delegates may inquire, on the oath of witnesses, into all complaints, grievances and offences, as the Grand Inquest of the State, and may commit any person for any crime to the public jail, there to remain until discharged by due course of law—they may examine and pass all accounts of the State, relating either to the collection or expenditure of the revenue, and appoint auditors to state and adjust the same—they may call for all public or official papers, and records, and send for persons whom they may judge necessary in the course of their inquiries concerning affairs relating to the public interest, and may direct all office bonds which shall be made payable to the State, to be sued for any breach of duty.

Provision for vacancies in office of Senator or Delegate.

SEC. 29. In case of death, disqualification, resignation, refusal to act, expulsion or removal from the county or city for which he shall have been elected, of any person who shall have been chosen as a Delegate or Senator, or in case of a tie between two or more such qualified persons, a warrant of election shall be issued by the Speaker of the House of Delegates or President of the Senate, as the case may be, for the election of another person in his place, of which election, not less than ten days notice shall be given, exclusive of the day of the publication of the notice and of the day of election; and in case of such resignation or refusal to act, being communicated in writing, to the Governor, by the person making it, or if such death occur during the legislative recess and more than ten days before its termination, it shall be the duty of the Governor to issue a warrant of election to supply the vacancy thus created in the same manner that the said Speaker or President might have done during the session of the Legislature; provided, however, that unless a meeting of the General Assembly may intervene, the election thus ordered to fill such vacancy shall be held on the day of the ensuing election for Delegates and Senators.

SEC. 30. The Senators and Delegates shall receive a per diem of four dollars, and such mileage as may be allowed by law, and the presiding officer of each House shall be allowed an addition of one dollar per day. No book or other printed matter not appertaining to the business of the session, shall be purchased or subscribed for, for the use of the members or be distributed among them, at the public expense. *Compensation of Senators and Delegates.*

Books not to be purchased.

SEC. 31. No law passed by the General Assembly shall take effect until the first day of June next after the session at which it may be passed, unless it be otherwise expressly declared therein. *When Laws to take effect.*

SEC. 32. No law shall be passed creating the office of Attorney General. *Office of Attorney General abolished.*

SEC. 33. The General Assembly shall have full power to exclude from the privilege of voting at elections, or of holding any civil or mili- *General Assembly may disfranchise certain persons.*

tary office in this State, any person who may thereafter be convicted of perjury, bribery, or other felony, unless such person shall have been pardoned by the Executive.

Mode of Attesting Laws.

SEC. 34. Every bill, when passed by the General Assembly, and sealed with the Great Seal, shall be presented to the Governor, who shall sign the same in the presence of the presiding officers and chief clerks of the Senate and House of Delegates. Every law shall be recorded in the office of the Court of Appeals, and in due time be printed, published and certified under the Great Seal to the several courts in the same manner as has been heretofore usual in this State.

Laws to be Recorded and certified to Courts.

Defaulting Collectors to be ineligible as Senators or Delegates.

SEC. 35. No person who may hereafter be a collector, receiver or holder of public moneys, shall be eligible as Senator or Delegate, or to any office of profit or trust under this State, until he shall have accounted for and paid into the treasury all sums on the books thereof, charged to and due by him.

Duellists ineligible to office.

SEC. 36. Any citizen of this State who shall, after the adoption of this Constitution, either in or out of this State, fight a duel with deadly weapons, or send or accept a challenge so to do, or who shall act as a second, or knowingly aid or assist in any manner those thus offending, shall ever thereafter be incapable of holding any office of trust or profit under this State.

Lotteries prohibited.

SEC. 37. No lottery grant shall ever hereafter be authorized by the Legislature.

Wife's property to be protected. 1853 ch. 245. 1853, ch. 335.

SEC. 38. The General Assembly shall pass laws necessary to protect the property of the wife, from the debts of the husband during her life, and for securing the same to her issue after her death.

SEC. 39. Laws shall be passed by the Legislature to protect from execution a reasonable amount of property of a debtor, not exceeding in value the sum of five hundred dollars. *Exemption Laws*

SEC. 40. The Legislature shall, at its first session after the adoption of this Constitution, adopt some simple and uniform system of charges in the offices of clerks of courts and registers of wills in the counties of this State and the city of Baltimore, and for the collection thereof; provided, the amount of compensation to any of said officers shall not exceed the sum of twenty-five hundred dollars a year, over and above office expenses, and compensation to assistants; and provided, further, that such compensation of clerks, registers, assistants and office expenses, shall always be paid out of the fees or receipts of the offices respectively. *Compensation of Clerks and Registers. 1852. ch. 308.*

SEC. 41. The House of Delegates shall have the sole power of impeachment in all cases, but a majority of all the members must concur in an impeachment; all impeachments shall be tried by the Senate, and when sitting for that purpose they shall be on oath or affirmation to do justice according to the law and evidence, but no person shall be convicted without the concurrence of two-thirds of all the Senators. *Impeachment.*

SEC. 42. That it shall be the duty of the Legislature so soon as the public debt shall have been fully paid off, to cause to be transferred to the several counties and the city of Baltimore, stock in the internal improvement *Internal Improvement Companies.*

companies, equal to the amount respectively paid by each towards the erection and completion of said works, at the then market value of said stock.

<small>Master and Slave</small>

SEC. 43. The Legislature shall not pass any law abolishing the relation of master or slave, as it now exists in this State.

<small>No Imprisonment for Debt.
5 Md. 337.</small>

SEC. 44. No person shall be imprisoned for debt.

<small>Banks not to be chartered.
1853, ch. 441.
1854, ch. 152.

Provisions relating to Banks.</small>

SEC. 45. The Legislature hereafter shall grant no charter for banking purposes or renew any banking corporation now in existence, except upon the condition that the stockholders and directors shall be liable to the amount of their respective share or shares of stock in such banking institution for all its debts and liabilities upon note, bill or otherwise; and upon the further condition that no director or other officer of said corporation shall borrow any money from said corporation; and if any director or other officer shall be convicted upon indictment of directly or indirectly violating this article, he shall be punished by fine or imprisonment at the discretion of the Court. All banks shall be open to inspection of their books, papers and accounts, under such regulations as may be prescribed by law.

<small>Private Property taken for Public use to be paid for.</small>

SEC. 46. The Legislature shall enact no law authorizing private property to be taken for public use without just compensation as agreed upon between the parties or awarded by a jury, being first paid or tendered to the party entitled to such compensation.

<small>Corporations to be provided for by General Laws.</small>

SEC. 47. Corporations may be formed under general laws, but shall not be created by spe-

cial act, except for municipal purposes, and in cases where, in the judgment of the Legislature, the object of the corporation cannot be attained under general laws. All laws and special acts pursuant to this section may be altered from time to time, or repealed; *provided*, nothing herein contained shall be construed to alter, change or amend in any manner the article in relation to Banks. _{1852, ch. 231.} _{1853, ch. 320.}

SEC. 48. The Legislature shall make provision for all cases of contested elections of any of the officers not herein provided for. _{Contested Elections.} _{1853, ch. 244.}

SEC. 49. That the rate of interest in this State shall not exceed six per cent. per annum, and no higher rate shall be taken or demanded, and the Legislature shall provide, by law, all necessary forfeitures and penalties against usury. _{Rate of Interest.}

ARTICLE IV.

JUDICIARY DEPARTMENT.

SECTION 1. The Judicial power of this State shall be vested in a Court of Appeals, in Circuit Courts, in such Courts for the city of Baltimore as may be hereinafter prescribed, and in Justices of the Peace. _{The Judicial Power—how vested.}

SEC. 2. The Court of Appeals shall have appellate jurisdiction only, which shall be coextensive with the limits of the State. It shall consist of a chief justice and three associate justices, any three of whom shall form a quorum, whose judgment shall be final and conclusive in all cases of appeals; and who shall _{Court of Appeals, its jurisdiction and constitution.}

have the jurisdiction which the present Court of Appeals of this State now has, and such other appellate jurisdiction as hereafter may be provided for by law. And in every case decided, an opinion, in writing, shall be filed, and provision shall be made, by law, for publishing reports of cases argued and determined in the said Court. The Governor, for the time being, by and with the advice and consent of the Senate, shall designate the chief justice, and the Court of Appeals shall hold its sessions at the city of Annapolis, on the first Monday of June, and the first Monday of December, in each and every year.

<small>Reports of Decisions to be published.
1852, ch. 55.
do. 351.
1854, Res. 5.
Time and place of meeting.</small>

<small>Clerk of Court of Appeals.</small>

SEC. 3. The Court of Appeals shall appoint its own clerk, who shall hold his office for six years, and may be re-appointed at the end thereof; he shall be subject to removal by the said court for incompetency, neglect of duty, misdemeanor in office, and for such other causes as may be prescribed by law.

<small>State divided into four Judicial Districts.</small>

SEC. 4. The State shall be divided into four Judicial districts: Allegany, Washington, Frederick, Carroll, Baltimore and Harford counties, shall compose the first; Montgomery, Howard, Anne Arundel, Calvert, St. Mary's, Charles and Prince George's, the second; Baltimore city, the third; and Cecil, Kent, Queen Anne's, Talbot, Caroline, Dorchester, Somerset and Worcester, shall compose the fourth district. And one person from among those learned in the law, having been admitted to practice in this State, and who shall have been a citizen of this State at least five years, and above the age of thirty years at the time of his

<small>One Judge of Court of Appeals to be elected from each district.
His Qualifications.</small>

election, and a resident of the judicial district, shall be elected from each of said districts by the legal and qualified voters therein, as a Judge of the said Court of Appeals, who shall hold his office for the term of ten years from the time of his election, or until he shall have attained the age of seventy years, which ever may first happen, and be re-eligible thereto until he shall have attained the age of seventy years, and not after, subject to removal for incompetency, wilful neglect of duty or misbehaviour in office, on conviction in a court of law, or by the Governor upon the address of the General Assembly, two-thirds of the members of each House concurring in such address; and the salary of each of the Judges of the Court of Appeals shall be two thousand five hundred dollars annually, and shall not be increased or diminished during their continuance in office; and no fees or perquisites of any kind shall be allowed by law to any of the said Judges. *1852, ch. 82. Term of Office. Salary. 1 Md. 368.*

SEC. 5. No judge of the Court of Appeals shall sit in any case wherein he may be interested, or where either of the parties may be connected with him by affinity or consanguinity within such degrees as may be prescribed by law, or when he shall have been of counsel in said case; when the Court of Appeals, or any of its members shall be thus disqualified to hear and determine any case or cases in said court, so that by reason thereof no judgment can be rendered in said court, the same shall be certified to the Governor of the State, who shall immediately commission the requisite *Judges of Court of Appeals disqualified in certain cases. 1852, ch. 263. Governor to appoint others to try such cases.*

number of persons learned in the law for the trial and determination of said case or cases.

<small>Judges to be conservators of the Peace.</small>

SEC. 6. All Judges of the Court of Appeals, of the Circuit Courts, and of the Courts for the city of Baltimore, shall, by virtue of their offices, be conservators of the peace throughout the State.

<small>Style of Commissions, Writs, Indictments, &c.</small>

SEC. 7. All public commissions and grants shall run thus: "The State of Maryland," &c., and shall be signed by the Governor, with the Seal of the State annexed; all writs and process shall run in the same style, and be tested, sealed and signed as usual; and all indictments shall conclude "against the peace, government and dignity of the State."

<small>State divided into eight Judicial Circuits.</small>

SEC. 8. The State shall be divided into eight Judicial Circuits, in manner and form following, to wit: St. Mary's, Charles and Prince George's counties shall be the first; Anne Arundel, Howard, Calvert and Montgomery counties shall be the second; Frederick and Carroll counties shall be the third; Washington and Allegany counties shall be the fourth; Baltimore city shall be the fifth; Baltimore, Harford and Cecil counties shall be the sixth; Kent, Queen Anne's, Talbot and Caroline counties shall be the seventh; and Dorchester, Somerset and Worcester counties shall be the

<small>One Judge to be elected for each Circuit.</small>

eighth; and there shall be elected as hereinafter directed for each of the said judicial circuits, except the fifth, one person from among those learned in the law, having been admitted

<small>His Qualifications.</small>

to practice in this State, and who shall have been a citizen of this State at least five years, and above the age of thirty years at the time of his election, and a resident of the judicial circuit, to be Judge thereof; the said Judges shall be styled Circuit Judges, and shall respectively hold a term of their courts at least twice in each year, or oftener if required by law, in each county composing their respective circuits; and the said courts shall be called Circuit Courts for the county in which they may be held, and shall have and exercise in the several counties of this State, all the power, authority and jurisdiction which the county courts of this State now have and exercise, or which may hereafter be prescribed by law, and the said Judges in their respective circuits, shall have and exercise all the power, authority and jurisdiction of the present Court of Chancery of Maryland; *Provided*, nevertheless, that Baltimore County Court may hold its sittings within the limits of the city of Baltimore, until provision shall be made by law for the location of a county seat within the limits of the said county proper, and the erection of a court house and all other appropriate buildings, for the convenient administration of justice in said court.

_{Terms of the Courts.}
_{1852, ch. 34.}
_{do. 46.}
_{do. 50.}
_{do. 51.}
_{do. 74.}
_{do. 95.}
_{do. 154.}
_{do. 214.}
_{do. 215.}
_{1853, ch. 198.}
_{do. 242.}
_{do. 243.}
_{1854, ch. 19.}
_{do. 135.}

_{Jurisdiction.}
_{1852, ch. 16.}
_{do. 31.}
_{do. 75.}
_{do. 111.}
_{do. 136.}
_{do. 219.}
_{do. 336.}
_{do. 344.}
_{1853, ch. 181.}
_{do. 238.}
_{do. 406.}
_{2 Md., 274.}

_{Baltimore County Court.}

_{1852, ch. 17.}
_{do. 18.}
_{do. 86.}

SEC. 9. The judges of the several judicial circuits shall be citizens of the United States, and shall have resided five years in this State, and two years in the judicial circuit for which they may be respectively elected, next before the time of their election, and shall reside therein while they continue to act as judges; they shall be taken from among those who having the other qualifications herein prescribed, are most distinguished for integrity, wis-

_{Qualifications of Judges of Circuit Courts.}

dom and sound legal knowledge, and shall be elected by the qualified voters of the said circuits, and shall hold their offices for the term of ten years, removable for misbehaviour, on conviction in a court of law or by the Governor, upon the address of the General Assembly, provided that two-thirds of the members of each House shall concur in such address, and the said judges shall each receive a salary of two thousand dollars a year, and the same shall not be increased or diminished during the time of their continuance in office; and no judge of any court in this State, shall receive any perquisite, fee, commission or reward, in addition thereto, for the performance of any judicial duty.

<small>Term of Office. 1 Md., 368. Salary.</small>

SEC. 10. There shall be established for the city of Baltimore one court of law, to be styled " the Court of Common Pleas," which shall have civil jurisdiction in all suits where the debt or damage claimed shall be over one hundred dollars, and shall not exceed five hundred dollars; and shall, also, have jurisdiction in all cases of appeal from the judgment of justices of the peace in the said city, and shall have jurisdiction in all applications for the benefit of the insolvent laws of this State, and the supervision and control of the trustees thereof.

<small>Court of Common Pleas. Its Jurisdiction. 1852, ch. 159. do. 251. 1853, ch. 238. 5 Md. 337.</small>

SEC. 11. There shall also be established, for the city of Baltimore, another court of law, to be styled "the Superior Court of Baltimore City," which shall have jurisdiction over all suits where the debt or damage claimed shall exceed the sum of five hundred dollars, and in case any plaintiff or plaintiffs shall recover less

<small>Superior Court. Its Jurisdiction. 1852, ch. 198. do. 227. do. 312. do. 323. 1853, ch. 451.</small>

than the sum or value of five hundred dollars, he or they shall be allowed or adjudged to pay costs in the discretion of the court. The said court shall also have jurisdiction as a Court of Equity within the limits of the said city, and in all other civil cases which have not been heretofore assigned to the Court of Common Pleas.

SEC. 12. Each of the said two courts shall consist of one judge, who shall be elected by the legal and qualified voters of the said city, and shall hold his office for the term of ten years, subject to the provisions of this Constitution, with regard to the election and qualification of judges and their removal from office, and the salary of each of the said judges shall be twenty-five hundred dollars a year; and the Legislature shall, whenever it may think the same proper and expedient, provide, by law, another court for the city of Baltimore, to consist of one judge to be elected by the qualified voters of the said city, who shall be subject to the same constitutional provisions, hold his office for the same term of years, and receive the same compensation as the judge of the Court of Common Pleas of the said city, and the said court shall have such jurisdiction and powers as may be prescribed by law. *Constitution of Baltimore Courts for civil cases. Qualification and Term of Office of the Judges. Their Salary. Another Court. 1853, ch. 122. do. 391.*

SEC. 13. There shall also be a Criminal Court for the city of Baltimore, to be styled "the Criminal Court of Baltimore," which shall consist of one judge, who shall also be elected by the legal and qualified voters of the said city, and who shall have and exercise all the jurisdiction now exercised by Baltimore City Court, and the said judge shall receive a salary of two *Criminal Court of Baltimore. 1853, ch. 33. Its Jurisdiction. 1852, ch. 344.*

thousand dollars a year and shall be subject to the provisions of this Constitution with regard to the election and qualifications of judges, term of office, and removal therefrom.

SEC. 14. There shall be in each county a Clerk of the Circuit Court, who shall be elected by the qualified voters of each county, and the person receiving the greatest number of votes shall be declared and returned duly elected Clerk of said Circuit Court for the said county, and shall hold his office for the term of six years from the time of his election, and until a new election is held; shall be re-eligible thereto, and subject to removal for wilful neglect of duty, or other misdemeanor in office, on conviction in a court of law. There shall also be a Clerk of the Court of Common Pleas in Baltimore city, and a Clerk of the Superior Court of Baltimore city, and there shall also be a Clerk of the Criminal Court of Baltimore city, and each of the said clerks shall be elected as aforesaid by the qualified voters of the city of Baltimore, and shall hold his office for six years from the time of his election, and until a new election is held, and be re-eligible thereto, subject, in like manner, to be removed for wilful neglect of duty or other misdemeanor in office, on conviction in a court of law. In case of a vacancy in the office of a clerk, the judge or judges of the court, of which he was clerk, shall have the power to appoint a clerk until the general election of delegates held next thereafter, when a clerk shall be elected to fill such vacancy.

SEC. 15. The Clerk of the Court of Common Pleas for Baltimore city, shall have authority to issue within the said city, all marriage and other licenses required by law, subject to such provisions as the Legislature shall hereafter prescribe; and the Clerk of the Superior Court for said city, shall have the custody of all deeds, conveyances, and other papers now remaining in the office of the clerk of Baltimore county court, and shall hereafter receive and record all deeds, conveyances, and other papers which are required by law to be recorded in said city. He shall also have the custody of all other papers connected with the proceedings on the law or equity side of Baltimore County Court, and of the dockets thereof, so far as the same have relation to Baltimore city.

<small>The respective Powers and Duties of the Clerks of the two Civil Courts in Baltimore City.
1853, ch. 86.</small>

SEC. 16. That the Clerk of the Court of Appeals, and the Clerks of the Circuit Courts in the several counties, shall respectively perform all the duties and be entitled to the fees which appertain to the offices of the Clerks of Court of Appeals for the Eastern and Western Shores and of the Clerks of County Courts, and the Clerks of the Court of Common Pleas, the Superior Court and the Criminal Court for Baltimore city, shall perform all the duties appertaining to their respective offices, and heretofore vested in the Clerks of Baltimore County Court and Baltimore City Court respectively, and be entitled to all the fees now allowed by law; and all laws relating to the Clerks of Court of Appeals, Clerks of the several County Courts and Baltimore City Court,

<small>Powers and Duties of the Clerks of Court of Appeals and Circuit Courts respectively.
1852, ch. 173.
do. 308.
1853, ch. 134.
do. 409.
do. 444.
1 Md. 374.</small>

shall be applicable to the Clerks respectively of the Court of Appeals, the Circuit Courts, the Court of Common Pleas, the Superior Court, and the Criminal Court of Baltimore City, until otherwise provided by law; and the said clerks, when duly elected and qualified according to law, shall have the charge and custody of the records and other papers belonging to their respective offices.

Judges of Orphans' Courts.

When and how to be elected.
1852, ch. 20.
do. 48.
do. 62.
do. 73.
do. 139.
do. 247.
do. 290.
do. 341.
1853, ch. 81.
do. 147.
do. 271.
do. 333.
do. 385.

Jurisdiction.

Compensation.

SEC. 17. The qualified voters of the city of Baltimore, and of the several counties of the State, shall, on the first Wednesday of November, eighteen hundred and fifty-one, and on the same day of the same month in every fourth year forever thereafter, elect three men to be Judges of the Orphans' Court of said city and counties respectively, who shall be citizens of the State of Maryland, and citizens of the city or county for which they may be severally elected at the time of their election. They shall have all the powers now vested in the Orphans' Courts of this State, subject to such changes therein as the Legislature may prescribe, and each of said Judges shall be paid at a per diem rate, for the time they are in session, to be fixed by the Legislature, and paid by the said counties and city respectively.

Register of Wills.

His Election.

Term of Office.

SEC. 18. There shall be a Register of Wills in each county of the State, and in the city of Baltimore, to be elected by the legal and qualified voters of said counties and city respectively, who shall hold his office for six years from the time of his election, and until a new election shall take place, and be re-eligible thereto, subject to be removed for wilful ne-

STATE OF MARYLAND. 51

glect of duty, or misdemeanor in office, in the same manner that the clerks of the county courts are removable. In the event of any vacancy in the office of Register of Wills, said vacancy shall be filled by the Judges of the Orphans' Court until the general election next thereafter for Delegates to the General Assembly, when a Register shall be elected to fill such vacancy. *Vacancies.*

SEC. 19. The Legislature at its first session after the adoption of this Constitution, shall fix the number of Justices of the Peace and Constables for each ward of the city of Baltimore, and for each election district in the several counties, who shall be elected by the legal and qualified voters thereof respectively, at the next general election for delegates thereafter, and shall hold their offices for two years from the time of their election, and until their successors in office are elected and qualified; and the Legislature may, from time to time, increase or diminish the number of Justices of the Peace and Constables to be elected in the several wards and election districts, as the wants and interests of the people may require. They shall be, by virtue of their offices, conservators of the peace in the said counties and city respectively, and shall have such duties and compensation as now exist, or may be provided for by law. In the event of a vacancy in the office of a justice of the peace, the Governor shall appoint a person to serve as justice of the peace, until the next regular election of said officers, and in case of a vacancy in the office of constable, the county com-

Number of Justices of the Peace and Constables to be fixed.
1852, ch. 274.

Their Election and Term of Office.

Number may be increased.
1853, ch. 102.
1854, ch. 302.

Duties and Compensation.
1852, ch. 76.
  do.   239.
1853, ch. 201.
1854, ch. 225.
  do.   236.

Vacancies.

missioners of the county, in which a vacancy may occur, or the Mayor and City Council of Baltimore, as the case may be, shall appoint a person to serve as constable until the next regular election thereafter for said officers. An appeal shall lie in all civil cases from the judgment of a Justice of the Peace to the Circuit Court, or to the Court of Common Pleas of Baltimore city, as the case may be, and on all such appeals, either party shall be entitled to a trial by jury, according to the laws now existing, or which may be hereafter enacted. And the Mayor and City Council may provide, by ordinance, from time to time, for the creation and government of such temporary additional police, as they may deem necessary to preserve the public peace.

SEC. 20. There shall be elected in each county and in the city of Baltimore, every second year, two persons for the office of sheriff for each county, and two for the said city, the one of whom having the highest number of votes of the qualified voters of said county or city, or if both have an equal number, either of them, at the discretion of the Governor, to be commissioned by the Governor for the said office, and, having served for two years, such persons shall be ineligible for the two years next succeeding; bond with security, to be taken every year, and no sheriff shall be qualified to act before the same be given. In case of death, refusal, disqualification or removal out of the county, before the expiration of the said two years, the other person chosen as aforesaid, shall be commissioned by the Governor to execute the said office for the residue of the said two years, the said person giving bond with security as aforesaid. No person shall be eligible to the office of sheriff but a resident of such county or city respectively, who shall have been a citizen of this State at least five years preceding his election, and above the age of twenty-one years. The two candidates, properly qualified, having the highest number of legal ballots, shall be declared duly elected for the office of sheriff for such county or city, and returned to the Governor, with a certificate of the number of ballots for each of them. *Qualifications.* *Returns of Elections.*

SEC. 21. Coroners, Elisors and Notaries Public shall be appointed for each county and the city of Baltimore, in the manner now prescribed by law, or in such other manner as the General Assembly may hereafter direct. *Coroners, Elisors and Notaries Public.*

SEC. 22. No Judge shall sit in any case wherein he may be interested, or where either of the parties may be connected with him by affinity, or consanguinity, within such degrees as may be prescribed by law, or where he shall have been of counsel in the case; and whenever any of the judges of the circuit courts, or of the courts of Baltimore city, shall be thus disqualified, or whenever, by reason of sickness, or any other cause, the said judges, or any of them, may be unable to sit in any cause, the parties may, by consent, appoint a proper person to try the said cause, or the judges, or any of them, shall do so when directed by law. *Judges disqualified from sitting in certain cases.* *1852, ch. 68. 1853, ch. 299. do. 425.* *Provisions for such cases and for sickness, &c.*

SEC. 23. The present Chancellor and the Register in Chancery, and, in the event of any *Provisions for abolishing the Court of Chancery.*

vacancy in their respective offices, their successors in office respectively, who are to be appointed as at present, by the Governor and Senate, shall continue in office, with the powers and compensation as at present established, until the expiration of two years after the adoption of this Constitution by the people, and until the end of the session of the Legislature next thereafter, after which the said offices of Chancellor and Register shall be abolished. The Legislature shall, in the mean time, provide by law for the recording, safekeeping, or other disposition, of the records, decrees, and other proceedings of the Court of Chancery, and for the copying and attestation thereof, and for the custody and use of the Great Seal of the State, when required, after the expiration of the said two years, and for transmitting to the said counties, and to the city of Baltimore, all the cases and proceedings in said Court then undisposed of and unfinished, in such manner, and under such regulations as may be deemed necessary and proper: *Provided*, that no new business shall originate in the said Court, nor shall any cause be removed to the same from any other court, from and after the ratification of this Constitution.

1854, ch. 149.

1853, ch. 131.
1854, ch. 81.

1853, ch. 123.
1854, ch. 183.

Time of Election of Judges, Clerks and Registers of Wills.

SEC. 24. The first election of Judges, Clerks, Registers of Wills, and all other officers, whose election by the people is provided for in this article of the Constitution, except justices of the peace and constables, shall take place throughout the State on the first Wednesday of November next after the ratification of this Constitution by the people.

STATE OF MARYLAND. 55

SEC. 25. In case of the death, resignation, removal, or other disqualification of a judge of any of the courts of law, the Governor, by and with the advice and consent of the Senate, shall thereupon appoint a person, duly qualified, to fill said office until the next general election for delegates thereafter; at which time an election shall be held as hereinbefore prescribed, for a judge, who shall hold the said office for ten years, according to the provisions of this Constitution. *Provisions in case of Death, &c., of Judges of Courts of Law.*

SEC. 26. In case of the death, resignation, removal, or other disqualification of the judge of an Orphans' Court, the vacancy shall be filled by the appointment of the Governor, by and with the advice and consent of the Senate. *Provisions in cases of Death, &c., of Judges of Orphans' Courts.*

SEC. 27. Whenever lands lie partly in one county, and partly in another, or partly in a county and partly in the city of Baltimore, or whenever persons proper to be made defendants to proceedings in Chancery, reside some in one county and some in another, that court shall have jurisdiction in which proceedings shall have been first commenced, subject to such rules, regulations and alterations as may be prescribed by law. *Jurisdiction in Chancery cases. 1852, ch. 16, sec. 5.*

SEC. 28. In all suits or actions at law, issues from the Orphans' Court or from any court sitting in equity, in petitions for freedom, and in all presentments and indictments now pending, or which may be pending at the time of the adoption of this Constitution by the people, or which may be hereafter instituted in any of the courts of law of this State, having jurisdiction thereof, the judge or judges there- *Removal of cases to an adjoining county. 1852, ch. 169. do. 315. 1854, ch. 325. 2 Md. 274. 5 Md. 370. 6 Md. 449.*

56   CONSTITUTION OF THE

How suggestions for removal to be made.

of, upon suggestion in writing, if made by the State's Attorney, or the prosecutor for the State, or upon suggestion in writing, supported by affidavit made by any of the parties thereto, or other proper evidence, that a fair and impartial trial cannot be had in the court where such suit or action at law, issues or petitions, or presentment and indictment is depending, shall order and direct the record of proceedings in such suit or action, issues or petitions, presentment or indictment, to be transmitted to the

To what County removals to be made.

court of any adjoining county; provided, that the removal in all civil causes be confined to an adjoining county within the judicial circuit, except as to the city of Baltimore, where the removal may be to an adjoining county, for trial, which court shall hear and determine the same in like manner as if such suit or action, issues or petitions, presentment or indictment, had been originally instituted therein; and *pro-*

When suggestions for removal to be made.

vided also, that such suggestion shall be made as aforesaid, before or during the term in which the issue or issues may be joined in said suit or action, issues or petition, presentment or indictment, and that such further remedy in the premises may be provided by law, as the Legislature shall from time to time direct and enact.

Elections and Returns thereof.

1853, ch. 134.

SEC. 29. All elections of judges, and other officers provided for by this Constitution, shall be certified, and the returns made by the clerks of the respective counties to the Governor, who shall issue commissions to the different persons for the offices to which they shall have been respectively elected; and in all such elections,

STATE OF MARYLAND. 57

the person having the greatest number of votes, shall be declared to be elected.

SEC. 30. If, in any case of election for Judges, Clerks of the Courts of Law and Registers of Wills, the opposing candidates shall have an equal number of votes, it shall be the duty of the Governor to order a new election; and in case of any contested election, the Governor shall send the returns to the House of Delegates, who shall judge of the election and qualification of the candidates at such election. *Cases of a tie and contested elections.*

SEC. 31. Every person of good moral character, being a voter, shall be admitted to practice law in all the courts of law in this State, in his own case. *Voters may plead their own cases.*

ARTICLE V.

THE STATE'S ATTORNEYS.

SECTION 1. There shall be an attorney for the State in each county and the city of Baltimore, to be styled "The State's Attorney," who shall be elected by the voters thereof, respectively, on the first Wednesday of November next, and on the same day every fourth year thereafter, and hold his office for four years from the first Monday of January next ensuing his election, and until his successor shall be elected and qualified, and shall be re-eligible thereto, and be subject to removal therefrom for incompetency, wilful neglect of duty or misdemeanor in office, on conviction in a court of law. *Election and Term of Office of the State's Attorneys.*

58   CONSTITUTION OF THE

<small>Returns of Elections to be made to Judges.</small>

SEC. 2. All elections for the State's Attorney shall be certified to, and returns made thereof, by the clerks of the said counties and city to the Judges thereof having criminal jurisdiction, respectively, whose duty it shall be to decide upon the elections and qualifications of the persons returned, and in case of a tie between two or more persons, to designate which of said persons shall qualify as State's Attorney, and to administer the oaths of office to the persons elected.

<small>Their Duties and their Fees.</small>

SEC. 3. The State's Attorney shall perform such duties and receive such fees and commissions as are now prescribed by law for the Attorney General and his Deputies, and such other duties, fees and commissions as may hereafter be prescribed by law, and if any State's Attorney shall receive any other fee or reward than such as is, or may be allowed by law, he shall, on conviction thereof, be removed from office.

<small>Their qualifications.</small>

SEC. 4. No person shall be eligible to the office of State's Attorney who has not been admitted to practice the law in this State, and who has not resided for at least one year in the county or city in which he may be elected.

<small>Vacancies.</small>

Sec. 5. In case of vacancy in the office of State's Attorney, or of his removal from the county or city in which he shall have been elected, or on his conviction as herein before specified, the said vacancy shall be filled by the Judge of the county or city, respectively, having criminal jurisdiction in which said vacancy shall occur, until the election and qualification of his successor; at which election

said vacancy shall be filled by the voters of the said county or city, for the residue of the term thus made vacant.

SEC. 6. It shall be the duty of the Clerk of the Court of Appeals, and the Commissioner of the Land Office, respectively, whenever a case shall be brought into said court or office, in which the State is a party, or has an interest, immediately to notify the Governor thereof. *State cases in Court of Appeals and Land Office.*

ARTICLE VI.

TREASURY DEPARTMENT.

SECTION 1. There shall be a Treasury Department, consisting of a Comptroller, chosen by the qualified electors of the State, at each election of members of the House of Delegates, who shall receive an annual salary of two thousand five hundred dollars; and of a Treasurer, to be appointed by the two Houses of the Legislature, at each session thereof, on joint ballot, who shall also receive an annual salary of two thousand five hundred dollars; and neither of the said officers shall be allowed or receive any fees, commissions, or perquisites of any kind, in addition to his salary, for the performance of any duty or service whatever. In case of a vacancy in either of the offices, by death or otherwise, the Governor, by and with the advice and consent of the Senate, shall fill such vacancy by appointment, to continue until another election by the people, or a choice by the Legislature, as the case may *Comptroller of the Treasury. His Election and Salary. 4 Md. 189. 1853, ch. 403. Treasurer. His Appointment and Salary. Vacancies.*

be, and the qualification of the successor. The Comptroller and the Treasurer shall keep their offices at the seat of government, and shall take such oath, and enter into such bonds, for the faithful discharge of their duties, as the Legislature shall prescribe.

<small>Place of their Offices.
Their Oaths and Bonds.
1852, ch. 12.</small>

SEC. 2. The Comptroller shall have the general superintendence of the fiscal affairs of the State: he shall digest and prepare plans for the improvement and management of the revenue, and for the support of the public credit; prepare and report estimates of the revenue and expenditure of the State; superintend and enforce the collection of all taxes and revenue; adjust, settle and preserve all public accounts; decide on the forms of keeping and stating accounts; grant, under regulations prescribed by law, all warrants for moneys to be paid out of the treasury, in pursuance of appropriations by law; prescribe the formalities of the transfer of stock or other evidences of the State debt; and countersign the same, without which such evidences shall not be valid; he shall make full reports of all his proceedings, and of the state of the Treasury Department within ten days after the commencement of each session of the Legislature, and perform such other duties as shall be prescribed by law.

<small>The Duties of the Comptroller of the Treasury.
1853, ch. 82, 83.
To prepare plans for Management of the Revenue.
To report estimates.
To superintend collections.
To adjust acc'ts.
To decide on the forms of accounts.
To grant warrants for moneys.
To regulate the transfer of stock.
1852, ch. 65.
To report all his proceedings to the Legislature.
1852, ch. 56.</small>

SEC. 3. The Treasurer shall receive and keep the moneys of the State, and disburse the same upon warrants drawn by the Comptroller, and not otherwise; he shall take receipts for all moneys paid by him, and all receipts for moneys received by him shall be endorsed upon warrants signed by the Comptroller, without

<small>The Duties of the Treasurer.
To receive and disburse moneys.
4 Md. 189.
To take receipts on the Comptroller's warrants.</small>

STATE OF MARYLAND. 61

which warrant, so signed, no acknowledgment of money received into the Treasury shall be valid; and upon warrants issued by the Comptroller he shall make arrangements for the payment of the interest of the public debt, and for the purchase thereof, on account of the sinking fund. Every bond, certificate, or other evidence of the debt of the State, shall be signed by the Treasurer and countersigned by the Comptroller, and no new certificate or other evidence intended to replace another shall be issued until the old one shall be delivered to the Treasurer, and authority executed in due form for the transfer of the same shall be filed in his office, and the transfer accordingly made on the books thereof, and the certificate or other evidence cancelled; but the Legislature may make provision for the loss of certificates or other evidence of the debt.

To provide for payment of Public Debt.

Provisions in relation to the evidences of the Public Debt.

1852, ch. 65. do. 123.

SEC. 4 The Treasurer shall render his accounts quarterly to the Comptroller; and on the third day of each session of the Legislature he shall submit to the Senate and House of Delegates fair and accurate copies of all accounts by him from time to time rendered and settled with the Comptroller. He shall at all times submit to the Comptroller the inspection of the moneys in his hands, and perform all other duties that shall be prescribed by law.

Treasurer to render accounts to the Comptroller quarterly and report to Legislature.

ARTICLE VII.

SUNDRY OFFICERS.

Commissioners of Public Works. SECTION 1. At the first general election of Delegates to the General Assembly, after the adoption of this Constitution, four Commissioners shall be elected as hereinafter provided, who shall be styled "Commissioners of Public *Their Duties.* Works," and who shall exercise a diligent and faithful supervision of all Public Works, in which the State may be interested as stockholder or creditor, and shall represent the State in all meetings of the Stockholders, and shall *To appoint Directors.* appoint the Directors in every Rail Road or Canal Company, in which the State has the constitutional power to appoint Directors. It shall also be the duty of the Commissioners of *To review and adjust Tolls.* Public Works to review, from time to time, the rate of tolls adopted by any company; use all legal powers which they may possess to obtain the establishment of rates of tolls, which may prevent an injurious competition with each other, to the detriment of the interests of the State; and so to adjust them as to promote the agriculture of the State. It shall also be the duty of the said Commissioners of Public *To keep a Journal.* Works to keep a journal of their proceedings; and at each regular session of the Legislature *To report to Legislature.* to make it a report, and to recommend such legislation as they shall deem necessary and requisite to promote or protect the interest of the State in the Public Works; and perform such other duties as may be prescribed by law. *Their Salary.* They shall each receive such salary as may be allowed by law, which shall not be increased or diminished during their continuance in office. 1852, ch. 122.

SEC. 2. For the election of the Commissioners of Public Works, the State shall be divided into four districts. The counties of Allegany, Washington, Frederick, Carroll, Baltimore and Harford, shall constitute the first district. The counties of Montgomery, Howard, Anne Arundel, Calvert, St. Mary's, Charles and Prince George's, shall constitute the second district. Baltimore city shall constitute the third district. The counties of Cecil, Kent, Queen Anne's, Talbot, Caroline, Dorchester, Somerset, and Worcester, shall constitue the fourth district. One commissioner shall be elected in each district, who shall have been a resident thereof at least five years next preceding his election. *State divided into four Districts.*

One Commissioner of Public Works to be elected in each. His qualifications.

SEC. 3. The said Commissioners shall be elected by the qualified voters of their districts respectively; the returns of their election shall be certified to the Governor, who shall, by proclamation, declare the result of the election. Two of the said commissioners, first elected, shall hold their office for four years, and the other two for two years from the first Monday of December next succeeding their election. And at the first meeting after their election, or as soon thereafter as practicable, they shall determine, by lot, who of their number shall hold their offices for four and two years respectively; and thereafter there shall be elected as aforesaid, at each general election of Delegates, two commissioners for the term of four years, to be taken from the districts respectively *The Returns of Elections of the Commissioners for Public Works*

Terms of Office.

wherein the commissioners resided at the time of their election, whose term of service has expired.

Vacancies.

And in case of a vacancy in the office of either of said commissioners, by death, resignation, or otherwise, the Governor, by and with the advice and consent of the Senate, shall appoint some qualified person from the same district, to serve until the next general election of Delegates, when an election shall be held, as aforesaid, for a commissioner for the residue of said term.

Case of a division of opinion.

And in case of an equal division in the board of commissioners, on any subject committed to their charge, the Treasurer of the State shall have power, and shall be called on to decide the same.

Cases of a Tie or of Contested Elections.

And in the event of a tie vote for any two of the candidates for the office of commissioner in the same district, it shall be the duty of the Governor to commission one or the other of the candidates having the equal number of votes. And if the Governor doubt the legality or result of any election held for said commissioners, it shall be his duty to send the returns of such election to the House of Delegates, who shall judge of the election and qualification of the candidates at such election.

Lottery Commissioner.
His Election.
1852, ch. 113.

SEC. 4. During the continuance of the lottery system in this State, there shall be elected by the legal and qualified voters of the State, at every general election for delegates to the General Assembly, one Commissioner of Lotteries, who shall hold his office for two years, and till the qualification of his successor, and shall be re-eligible.

Term of Office.

His Compensation.

His whole compensation shall be paid out of the fund raised for the Maryland Consolidated Lottery grants, and shall not exceed the amount of commissions received by one of the present Lottery Commissioners, out of said fund; and he shall give such bond, for the faithful performance of his duties as is now given by the Lottery Commissioners. The term of the Commissioner, who shall be elected at the general election for Delegates next succeeding the adoption of this Constitution, shall commence at the expiration of the commissions of the present Lottery Commissioners, and continue for two years, and till the qualification of his successor. *His Bond.*

SEC. 5. From and after the first day of April, eighteen hundred and fifty-nine, no lottery scheme shall be drawn, for any purpose whatever, nor shall any lottery ticket be sold in this State; and it shall be the duty of the several commissioners elected under this Constitution, to make such contract or contracts as will extinguish all existing lottery grants before the said first day of April, eighteen hundred and fifty-nine, and also secure to the State a clear yearly revenue equal to the average amount derived by the State from the system for the last five years; but no such contract or contracts shall be valid until approved by the Treasurer and Comptroller. *Provisions for abolishing Lotteries.*

SEC. 6. There shall be a Commissioner of the Land Office elected by the qualified voters of the State, at the first general election of Delegates to the Assembly after the ratification of this Constitution, who shall hold his office for the term of six years from the first day of January next after his election. The *Commissioner of the Land Office. His Election and Term of Office.*

returns of said election shall be made to the Governor, and in the event of a tie between any two or more candidates, the Governor shall direct a new election to be held by writs to the several sheriffs, who shall hold said election after at least twenty days notice, exclusive of the day of election. The said Commissioner shall sit as judge of the Land Office, and receive therefor the sum of two hundred dollars per annum, to be paid out of the State Treasury. He shall also perform the duties of the Register of the Land Office, and be entitled to receive therefor the fees now chargeable in said office; and he shall also perform the duties of Examiner General, and be entitled to receive therefor the fees now chargeable by said officer. The office of Register of the Land Office and Examiner General shall be abolished from and after the election and qualification of the Commissioner of the Land Office.

SEC. 7. The State Librarian shall be elected by the joint vote of the two branches of the Legislature, for two years, and until his successor shall be elected and qualified. His salary shall be one thousand dollars per annum. He shall perform such duties as are now or may hereafter be prescribed by law.

SEC. 8. The county authorities now known as Levy Courts or County Commissioners, shall hereafter be styled "County Commissioners," and shall be elected by general ticket, and not by districts, by the voters of the several counties, on the first Wednesday in November, one thousand eight hundred and fifty-one, and on the same day in every second year thereafter. Said Commissioners shall exercise such powers and duties only as the Legislature may from time to time prescribe; but such powers and duties, and the tenure of office, shall be uniform throughout the State, and the Legislature shall, at or before its second regular session, after the adoption of this Constitution, pass such laws as may be necessary for determining the number for each county, and ascertaining and defining the powers, duties, and tenure of office of said Commissioners; and until the passage of such laws the Commissioners elected under this Constitution shall have and exercise all the powers and duties in their respective counties, now exercised by the county authorities under the laws of the State.

Their Powers and Duties to be uniform throughout the State.

Their Number and Powers and Term of Office to be fixed by the Legislature.

1853, ch. 173.
do. 220.
do. 239.
do. 372.
6 Md. 468.

SEC. 9. The General Assembly shall provide by law for the election of Road Supervisors, in the several counties, by the voters of the election districts respectively, and may provide by law for the election or appointment of such other county officers as may be required, and are not herein provided for, and prescribe their powers and duties; but the tenure of office, their powers and duties, and mode of appointment, shall be uniform throughout the State.

Supervisors of Roads and other officers.

1853, ch. 300.

Provision for their Election, &c., to be made by Legislature.

SEC. 10. The qualified voters of each county, and the city of Baltimore, shall, at the first election of delegates after the adoption of this Constitution, and every two years thereafter, elect a Surveyor for the counties, and the city of Baltimore respectively, whose duties and compensation shall be the same as are now prescribed by law for the county and city Sur-

Surveyors. Their Election and Term of office.

Their Duties and Compensations.

1852, ch. 59.

veyors respectively, or as may hereafter be prescribed by law. The term of office of said county and city Surveyors respectively, shall commence on the first Monday of January next succeeding their election. And vacancies in said office of Surveyors, by death, resignation or removal from their respective counties or city, shall be filled by the Commissioners of the counties, or Mayor and City Council of Baltimore respectively.

Commencement of their Term of Office.

Vacancies.

Wreck-Master. His Election and Term of Office.

SEC. 11. The qualified voters of Worcester county shall, at the first election of delegates after the adoption of this Constitution, and every two yers thereafter, elect a Wreck-Master for the said county, whose duties and compensation shall be the same as are now prescribed or may be hereafter prescribed by law. The term of office of said Wreck-Master shall commence on the first Monday of January next succeeding his election; and a vacancy in said office, by death, resignation, or removal from the county, shall be filled by the county commissioners of said county, for the residue of the term thus made vacant.

His Duties and Compensation.

Commencement of his Term of Office.

Vacancies.

ARTICLE VIII.

NEW COUNTIES.

Howard County created.

1 Md. 139.

SECTION 1. That part of Anne Arundel county called Howard District, is hereby erected into a new county, to be called Howard county, the inhabitants whereof shall have, hold and enjoy all such rights and privileges as are held and enjoyed by the inhabitants of the other counties in this State; and its civil and municipal officers, at the time of the ratification of this Constitution, shall continue in office until their successors shall have been elected or appointed, and shall have qualified as such; and all rights, powers and obligations incident to Howard District of Anne Arundel county shall attach to Howard county.

SEC. 2. When that part of Allegany county, lying south and west of a line beginning at the summit of Big Back Bone or Savage Mountain, where that mountain is crossed by Mason and Dixon's line, and running thence by a straight line, to the middle of Savage river where it empties into the Potomac river, thence by a straight line, to the nearest point or boundary of the State of Virginia; then with said boundary to the Fairfax stone, shall contain a population of ten thousand, and the majority of electors thereof shall desire to separate and form a new county, and make known their desire by petition to the Legislature, the Legislature shall direct at the next succeeding election, that the Judges shall open a book at each Election district in said part of Allegany county, and have recorded therein the vote of each elector "For or Against" a new county. In case the majority are in favor, then said part of Allegany county to be declared an independent county, and the inhabitants whereof shall have, and enjoy all such rights and privileges as are held and enjoyed by the inhabitants of the other counties in this State. *Provided*, that the whole representation in the Ge-

Provisions for creating a new County out of part of Allegany County.

neral Assembly of the county, when divided, shall not exceed the present delegation of Allegany county, allowed under this Constitution until after the next census.

ARTICLE IX.

MILITIA.

<small>Enrolment of Militia.</small>

<small>Districting the State.</small>

<small>Encouraging Volunteers.</small>
<small>1853, ch. 343.</small>

<small>Election of Officers.</small>

<small>The Adjutant General.</small>
<small>2 Md. 341.</small>
<small>His Term of Office and Salary.</small>

SECTION 1. It shall be the duty of the Legislature to pass laws for the enrolment of the militia; to provide for districting the State into divisions, brigades, battalions, regiments, and companies, and to pass laws for the effectual encouragement of volunteer corps by some mode which may induce the formation and continuance of at least one volunteer company in every county and division in the city of Baltimore. The company, battalion, and regimental officers (staff officers excepted) shall be elected by the persons composing their several companies, battalions and regiments.

SEC. 2. The Adjutant General shall be appointed by the Governor, by and with the advice and consent of the Senate. He shall hold his office for the term of six years, and receive the same salary as heretofore, until changed by the Legislature.

ARTICLE X.

MISCELLANEOUS.

SECTION 1. Every officer of this State, the Governor excepted, the entire amount of whose pay or compensation received for the discharge of his official duties shall exceed the yearly sum of three thousand dollars, shall keep a book, in which shall be entered every sum or sums of money received by him or on his account as a payment or compensation for his performance of official duties, a copy of which entries in said book, verified by the oath of the officer by whom it is directed to be kept, shall be returned yearly to the Treasurer of the State for his inspection and that of the General Assembly of Maryland; and each of such officers, when the amount received by him for the year shall exceed the sum of three thousand dollars, shall yearly pay over to the treasurer the amount of such excess by him received, subject to such disposition thereof as the Legislature may deem just and equitable. And any such officer failing to comply with the said requisition, shall be deemed to have vacated his office, and be subject to suit by the State for the amount that ought to have been paid into the treasury.

Compensation of Officers not to exceed $3,000.
1853, ch. 444.
1854, ch. 196.

The excess of fees, &c., to be paid to Treasurer.

On failure, their Offices vacated.

SEC. 2. The Legislature shall have power to pass all such laws as may be necessary and proper for carrying into execution the powers vested by this Constitution, in any department or office of the government, and the duties imposed upon them thereby.

Legislature to pass laws to carry out the provisions of the Constitution.
1852, ch. 172.

72 CONSTITUTION OF THE

In case of a tie in Election, a new one to be ordered.
1854, ch. 26.

SEC. 3. If in any election directed by this Constitution any two or more candidates shall have the highest and an equal number of votes, a new election shall be ordered, unless in cases specially provided for by the Constitution.

Trial by Jury preserved in cases over five dollars.

SEC. 4. The trial by jury of all issues of fact in civil proceeding, in the several courts of law in this State, where the amount in controversy exceeds the sum of five dollars, shall be inviolably preserved.

Jury to be Judges of Law and Fact in Criminal cases.

SEC. 5. In the trial of all criminal cases the jury shall be the judges of law as well as fact.

Legislature to regulate Elections.
1852, ch. 183.
1853, ch. 134.

SEC. 6. The Legislature shall have power to regulate by law all matters which relate to the judges, time, place and manner of holding elections in this State, and of making returns thereof, provided that the tenure and term of office, and the day of election shall not be affected thereby.

Vested Rights, &c., to remain.
1 Md. 368.

SEC. 7. All rights vested, and all liabilities incurred shall remain as if this Constitution had not been adopted.

Governor and other officers to continue in Office.
1 Md. 140.
do. 368.
2 Md. 341.

SEC. 8. The Governor and all officers, civil and military, now holding commissions under this State, shall continue to hold and exercise their offices, according to their present tenure, until they shall be superseded, pursuant to the provisions of this Constitution, and until their successors be duly qualified.

Sheriffs to give notice of the Elections.

SEC. 9. The sheriffs of the several counties of this State, and of the city of Baltimore, shall give notice of the several elections authorized by this Constitution, in the manner prescribed by existing laws for elections under the present Constitution.

STATE OF MARYLAND. 73

SEC. 10. This Constitution, if adopted by a majority of the legal votes cast on the first Wednesday of June next, shall go into operation on the fourth day of July next, and on and after said day shall supersede the present Constitution of this State. *This Constitution to go into effect on 4th July.*

ARTICLE XI.

AMENDMENT OF THE CONSTITUTION.

It shall be the duty of the Legislature, at its first session immediately succeeding the returns of every census of the United States, hereafter taken, to pass a law for ascertaining, at the next general election of Delegates, the sense of the people of Maryland in regard to the calling a Convention for altering the Constitution; and in case the majority of votes cast at said election shall be in favor of calling a Convention, the Legislature shall provide for assembling such Convention, and electing Delegates thereto at the earliest convenient day; and the Delegates to the said Convention shall be elected by the several counties of the State and the city of Baltimore, in proportion to their representation respectively in the Senate and House of Delegates, at the time when said Convention may be called. *The sense of the people to be taken every ten years in regard to calling a Convention for altering the Constitution.* *The Proportion of Delegates to such Convention.*

10

Done in Convention the 13*th day of May, in the year of our Lord one thousand eight hundred and fifty-one, and of the Independence of the United States the seventy-fifth.*

J. G. CHAPMAN,
President of the Convention.

Attest—GEORGE G. BREWER,
　　Secretary to Convention.

STATE OF MARYLAND,
　　COURT OF APPEALS, W. S.

I, RICHARD W. GILL, *Clerk of the Court of Appeals aforesaid, do hereby certify that this Constitution was this sixteenth day of May, in the year of our Lord eighteen hundred and fifty-one, filed in this office.—Witness my hand as Clerk.*

R. W. GILL, *Clerk.*

APPENDIX TO SECOND EDITION.

HAVING, at the request of the publishers, prepared the marginal notes to this Edition of the New Constitution, it seemed to me that it would be useful to add, by way of Appendix, brief notes of the principal changes which have been made in the fundamental law of the State, with their apparent or supposed causes, and of the subjects that require particular attention on the part of the Legislature, and of officers in other departments of the Government.

It is said, by the learned and elegant Commentator on the Laws of England, that there are three points to be considered in the construction of statutes, viz. the old law, the mischief and the remedy. The framers of the New Constitution had before them the Old Law, and had also, it is to be presumed, some idea of the mischiefs, which were intended to be prevented, by the remedies which have been provided. It may be useful therefore to note both the changes and their causes; for no change is ever made without a cause, and without a due consideration of both, no man can clearly understand or properly perform his duty.

THE DECLARATION OF RIGHTS.

This Declaration, consisting principally of immutable principles of government, has been but slightly altered.

The addition to the *first article* of it is the only change of sufficient importance to notice. It relates to the "unalienable right to alter the form of government," and contains a restriction of this right to "the mode prescribed in the Constitution." The importance of this alteration may be seen by reflection upon the fact that the Old Constitution was altered, at the time of the formation of this New one, in a mode different from that which was prescribed in the former, and that the right of alteration in the new mode was, at that time, the subject of much discussion.

THE CONSTITUTION.

Art. I.—Elective Franchise.

The Elective Franchise, which is the subject of the *first article* of the New Constitution, has been a little enlarged, by the provision in relation to removals; and it is moreover better protected than heretofore, by the provisions against fraud. The oath, which is now required of all officers, before entering upon their duties, that they have not been in any way guilty of bribery at elections, and the perpetual disfranchisement of those who have at any time violated the laws regulating the elective franchise, are important and salutary changes. The whole foundation of a Republican Government is the will of the people fairly expressed, and all attempts to influence that will, by any other means than rational argument, tend to the destruction of that form of government, and hence of Liberty.

Art. II.—Executive Department.

By the *first section* of this article the term of office of the Governor is enlarged from three to four years. By this change, the expiration of it is made to coincide with that of every second term of the Delegates, they being elected biennially, in which respect there is a similarity between the Constitution of this State and that of the United States.

By the *fourth section* it is provided, that when two or more persons have the highest and an equal number of votes for Governor, the second vote shall be confined to those persons, and if the votes be again equal, the election is to be determined by lot. The great use of such a provision, in some cases, will readily be perceived by those who have studied the history of the elections of Speakers, Presidents and other officers, both in the National and State Legislatures. It would have been well if this principle had been extended to other officers than the Governor. It can be demonstrated, with almost mathematical certainty, that the only plan which is both just and certain in its operation, for the election of a person to any office, where there are several candidates, is continually to drop the lowest one, after the first ballot, and if at last there be a tie, to decide by lot.

The *ninth section* prohibits the Governor from taking the command in person of the forces of the State, without the consent of the Legislature. It is to be hoped that there may never be occasion for his asking or their giving such consent.

APPENDIX. 77

The *seventeenth section* imposes upon the Governor the new duty of examining the books of the Treasurer, which is designed to be an additional check upon that Department of Government.

The *nineteenth section* imposes restrictions upon the pardoning power, which are well calculated to restrain the exercise of it within proper bounds.

Besides these changes, affecting the Governor's prerogative, there is another, which is the most *important* of them all. He has been stripped of the power of judging of the suitability of candidates for all the principal offices in the State, and of appointing them, by and with the advice and consent of the Senate, and is now clothed with such powers only as properly appertain to the chief Executive authority in a State. It is to be presumed that several causes operated together to produce this change, viz. with some persons, a conviction that the Legislative, Executive and Judicial powers of the government were not separate and distinct from each other, under the old mode of appointing Judges, &c.—although the Declaration of Rights expressly declares that they ought to be;—with others, an opinion that the people at large can judge of the qualifications of candidates for all offices as well as the Governor can; and with a third class of persons, a disposition to restrain the appointing power of the Governor, or the Executive patronage, as it is called, in order to prevent what was thought to be its injurious influence upon popular elections, and its growing tendency to abuse.

Art. III.—Legislative Department.

The changes which have been made in this Article are numerous and important.

By the *second section* of it the term of office of Senators is reduced from six to four years, and by a subsequent section it is provided, that one-half of them, instead of one-third as formerly, shall be elected biennially. The Old Constitution, in this respect, was like that of the United States, but it was contended, by those who advocated this change, that the term was so long as in a measure to take away the responsibility of Senators to the people for their conduct.

The *third section* apportions representation in the House of Delegates according to population. This principle of representation, now for the first time adopted in this State, although it is a fundamental one in all Republican governments, is restricted in regard to Baltimore City, for fear that her power might become so great as to lead to the passing of laws, either for her own particular benefit, or for the oppression of the Counties.

By the *seventh section*, the regular sessions of the Legislature are a little shortened, by changing the time of meeting. The first two Sessions after the adoption of this Constitution are excepted. It will be observed that, by subsequent provisions, the Legislature will be prevented from occupying its time by the enactment of many local and private laws.

The *fourteenth* and *fifteenth sections* will give greater publicity to the proceedings of the Legislature.

The *seventeenth section* embraces some of the most useful provisions that are to be found in the whole Constitution. It relates to the manner of passing laws, to their revision and codification, to the manner of amending the code after it is adopted, and to the simplification and abridgment of the rules of Practice, Pleading, Conveyancing, &c. This State has long been suffering for want of a proper codification of its laws. Several attempts indeed have been made, both with and without the aid of the Legislature, but all of them have proved to be failures; and a great and lasting benefit will be conferred upon the people, if the Commissioners for revision faithfully fulfil the duties assigned to them. While several of our sister States have, for many years past, enjoyed the advantage of a well arranged system of laws, framed to suit their advanced state of civilization and liberty, we yet live under some that were framed more than a century ago, many of which have been abolished in England where they originated. The able Report of Mr. Kilty, made under the direction of the Legislature, shewing which of the British statutes are in force in Maryland, and which are proper to be incorporated into our Laws, will require the attention of the Commissioners for revision.

The *eighteenth section* takes away the restriction upon the Senate from originating money bills, upon the ground perhaps that, as the reason for such a restriction had ceased, the law itself should cease. The remaining part of this section and the *nineteenth section* contain new provisions to prevent laws being passed in too great haste, or without the sanction of a majority of the members of the Legislature, the causes for which provisions may readily be found in the history of past legislation in this State.

The *twenty-first section* prohibits the Legislature from granting divorces, obviously because it would occupy too much time, and because it is properly a judicial act.

APPENDIX.   79

The *twentieth* and *twenty-second sections*, prohibiting the contracting of Public Debt, or the loan of the credit of the State, by the Legislature, will, it is to be hoped, prevent her fair name from being again tarnished, as it has been, by a failure to meet her pecuniary obligations to creditors at home and abroad. Honor as well in a State as in an individual, ought to be as zealously guarded as Liberty.

The *twenty-third section* prohibits extra compensation from being given, after a contract is made, as it has been often heretofore.

The *thirtieth section* fixes the per diem of members and prevents useless expenditures.

The *thirty-second section* abolishes the office of Attorney-General.

The *thirty-third section* provides for the protection of the Elective Franchise, further than is provided in the first article, by allowing certain criminals to be disfranchised.

The *thirty-sixth section*, making duelists ineligible to any office, will tend to check the practice of settling disputes by a most barbarous method.

The *thirty-eighth, thirty-ninth* and *forty-fourth sections* providing first, for the protection of a wife's property—second, for the exemption of a debtor's property to a certain amount—and third, for the abolishment of imprisonment for debt, will essentially alter the relations of debtor and creditor, and make the reliance upon personal character a more important element than heretofore in mercantile and other transactions, where the credit system prevails. These sections require the special attention of the Legislature.

The *fortieth section* imposes upon the Legislature the difficult but very necessary duty of adopting some simple and uniform system of charges in the offices of Clerks and Registers, and limits their compensation to twenty-five hundred dollars per annum. The charges heretofore fixed had, by change in the amount of business, and other circumstances, become too high, and the salaries of some of these officers had grown to be enormous.

The *forty-fifth* and *forty-seventh sections* contain provisions in relation to Banks and other corporations, which seem to be perfectly in accordance with the declaration (No. 39) "That monopolies are odious, contrary to the spirit of a free government, and to the principles of commerce, and ought not to be suffered."

The omission of the provision, contained in the Old Constitution, against a tax for religion, was made probably on the ground that in this enlightened age the Legislature did not need to be reminded of the impropriety of it.

Art. IV.—Judiciary Department.

The greatest changes in this Department are
1st. The substitution of a term of years for the life tenure of the Judges:
2d. The election of Judges, Clerks and Registers by the people:
3d. The substitution of one Judge for three in the County Courts:
4th. The abolishment of the Court of Chancery.

The two changes first named are owing to the prevalence of such opinions as are referred to in the comments on the Executive Department and on the change of the senatorial term of office; and the other two may safely be said to have been made principally from pecuniary considerations. Several duties are to be performed by the Legislature in relation to this department, which will be pointed out at the close of these notes.

Art. V.—State's Attorneys.

This article is entirely new. It was before observed that a change was made by abolishing the office of Attorney-General; and the provision that those officers who were formerly called his Deputies and were appointed by him, shall be elected by the people, is in harmony with other parts of the instrument.

Art. VI.—Treasury Department.

The whole of this department has been remodeled. The Comptroller of the Treasury is a new officer designed as a check upon the Treasurer. The former is to be elected by the people and the latter by the legislature. This plan of giving authority to one from one source, and to the other from another, makes them, in a measure, independent of each other; and thereby the danger of collusion is greatly lessened. By the old system there was no such check upon the Treasurer, the integrity of a single individual being the chief and almost the only safeguard of the State in regard to its treasure.

Art. VII.—Sundry Officers.

This article provides for the election of sundry officers by the people. The office of Commissioner of Public Works, of whom there are to be four, is a new one. Their duty is to superintend the interest of the State in Rail Road and Canal Companies.

APPENDIX. 81

By the *fourth* and *fifth sections* it is provided that a Lottery Commissioner shall be elected every two years until 1st April, 1859, when the whole system is to be abolished.

By the *sixth section* the Commissioner of the Land Office is to be elected by the people, and to perform the duties of the Register of the Land Office and Examiner-General.

The *eighth section* provides for the election of County Commissioners, and that their powers and duties shall be uniform throughout the State. This is a great improvement upon the existing Acts of Assembly in regard to those officers and their duties.

Art. VIII.—New Counties.

By this article one new county is created, and provision is made for the creation of another.

Art. IX.—Militia.

Sundry duties are here prescribed for the Legislature in regard to statutes to be passed for regulating the Militia of the State. The present law on the subject is not enforced, and it is comparatively a dead letter.

Art. X.—Miscellaneous.

Among the miscellaneous provisions in this article, those in the *first section* are particularly to be noted, as being new and useful, viz. that every officer, except the Governor, who receives more than three thousand dollars per annum, for the performance of his official duties, shall pay the balance into the Treasury, and give a statement of his receipts and expenditures. The fact that certain officers heretofore received compensations much too large, led to these provisions.

Art. XI.—Amendment of the Constitution.

By this article the mode of amending the Constitution has been entirely changed. The former mode was that amendments must be made by an Act of Assembly passed at one session and a conformatory Act at the next; but hereafter they are to be made by Conventions, elected for this purpose, at intervals of ten years. The principal arguments urged in favor of this latter mode are:—*first,* that the fundamental law of the State, being superior to all the departments of government, and regulating, among other things, the powers and duties of the Legislature itself, ought not to be under the control of the Legislature or any other department of the government, in order that the equilibrium, and the balances and checks, which have been provided to preserve the independence of the several departments, should not be destroyed, and that one department should not trespass upon the rights of another;—*secondly*, that the amendment of a Constitution, which is a work of more importance than the ordinary business of legislation, should not be mixed up with this, but be made at a time specially appointed for the purpose;—*thirdly*, that the Delegates to a Convention to amend the Constitution will be wiser and better men than those of the Legislature.

The Duties of the Legislature.

The duties imposed upon the Legislature, by the provisions of the New Constitution, being numerous and interspersed with various subjects throughout the instrument, it will facilitate references to all or any of them to note them in order.

Some of these duties are required either by the instrument itself, or from evident necessity, to be performed, *at the first session of the Legislature* after the adoption of it. These may be seen by reference to the following articles and sections, viz. :

Article 3, *sections* 6, 17, and 40.
Article 4, *sections* 10, 11, 12, 19, and 23.
Article 10, *sections* 2 and 6.

Other Duties of the Legislature are prescribed or referred to in the following, viz.:

Declaration of Rights, No. 41.
Art. 1, *section* 3.
Art. 2, *section* 8.
Art. 3, *sections* 33, 38, 39, 48, and 49.
Art. 4, *sections* 2, 8, 21, and 22.
Art. 7, *sections* 8 and 9.
Art. 9, *section* 1.

The author of these brief notes hopes that they may prove, what they are designed to be, some assistance or help to those who have special duties imposed upon them by the New Constitution, as well as to others who may wish to understand the changes it has produced in regard to their rights, civil and political.

EDWARD OTIS HINKLEY.

Baltimore, *Oct.* 11, 1851.

INDEX.

	PAGE
Abridgment of legal forms, &c.	33
Absentees, attendance of, may be compelled by Legislature.	31
Absurdity of the doctrine of non-resistance.	10
Accountability of public officers.	10
to God, belief in, a necessary qualification for a Witness or Juror.	16
Accusation, every man to be informed of, against him.	12
Action, not allowed for words spoken in debate.	36
removal of.	56
Acts, committed before retrospective laws.	12
moral accountability for.	16
record of, to be kept by Secretary of State.	27
Acts of Assembly, in force in Maryland.	10
relating to Annapolis.	17
Addition, to the code of laws to be published	33
to salary of Treasurer or Comptroller not allowed.	59
Address of General Assembly to remove Judges	14, 43, 46
Adjournment of the Legislature.	30, 31, 32
Adjustment of accounts of the State.	36, 60
Adjutant General to be appointed by Governor.	70
Administration of Justice, independency, &c., of Judges	14
of oath of office to State's Attorney.	58
Admission to practice law, of voters.	57
a qualification of State's Attorney.	58
Adoption of the Constitution.	9, 73
Advice, of Senate necessary to appointment of Judges, &c.	55, 59, 64, 70
Affinity of Judges to parties in cases.	43, 53
Age, of voters.	18
of Governor.	23
of Senator.	30
of Delegate.	31
of Judges.	42, 43, 44
of Sheriff.	53
Agents, no extra compensation to be allowed to.	35
Agriculture, to be encouraged by the Legislature.	17
tolls to be adjusted so as to promote.	62
Aids, not to be levied without consent of Legislature.	11
Alleghany Co., provisions about creating a new county.	69
Allegiance, oath of.	20
Allowance, additional not to be made to Public Officers.	35
to Senators and Delegates.	37

INDEX.

	PAGE
Allowance, to Clerks, of their fees	49
to State's Attorneys	58
to Treasurer and Comptroller	59
Alteration, of salaries not allowed	35
Amendment, of the Constitution	9, 10, 11, 17, 73
of bills, &c.	32, 33
Annapolis City, to be the place of meeting of Legislature	11
to have its charter rights, &c.	17
Court of Appeals to sit there	42
Appointments by the Governor	24, 25, 27
of Commissioners to Codify Laws and to revise Rules of Practice, &c.	32, 33
Senators and Delegates not to receive	35
by House of Delegates of Auditors	36
of Judge of Court of Appeals, in case of disqualification	43
of Clerks of Courts, to fill vacancies	48
of Registers of Wills, to fill vacancies	51
of Justices of the Peace, to fill vacancies	51
of Constables, to fill vacancies	51
of Sheriffs, to fill vacancies	52
of Coroners, to fill vacancies	53
of Judges, in case of disqualification	53
of Judges, to fill vacancies	55
of State's Attorneys, to fill vacancies	58
of Comptroller and Treasurer, to fill vacancies	59
of Directors of Rail Road and Canal Companies	62
of Commissioners of Public Works, to fill vacancies	64
of county officers to be provided for	67
of Surveyors, to fill vacancies	68
of Wreck-masters, to fill vacancies	68
of Adjutant-General	70
Apportionment of Delegates	28
Appropriations of money, how to be made by Legislature	33
of proceeds of internal improvement companies, &c., restrained	34
duties of Comptroller in relation to	60
Armies, standing, dangerous to liberty	14
Arrangement of code not to be altered by Legislature	33
for payment of interest on public debt to be made by Treasurer	61
Arrest of military officers for disobedience	25
members of General Assembly exempt from	35
Arts to be encouraged by Legislature	17
Assembly, Acts of, in force	10
to consist of two branches	28
to meet in January, biennially	30
address of two-thirds to remove Judges	46
Assessment of paupers not to be made	11
Attainder, laws of, not to be made	12
Attendance of absent members may be compelled by each House of Assembly	31
Attestation of Divine Being in administering oaths	17

INDEX.

	PAGE
Attestation of the laws of the State	38
of records of late Court of Chancery	54
Attorney-General, no law to be passed creating office of	37
Attorneys of the State, removal of cases upon suggestion of	56
their election, &c	57
Auditors of accounts of the State to be appointed by House of Delegates	36
Avoidance of sanguinary laws	12
Ayes—see *yeas*.	
Bail	13
Ballot	18, 22, 59
Baltimore City, representation of restricted	28
Courts and Clerks of	46, 47, 48, 49
Baltimore County, its county seat and court house	45
Bank book	26, 40, 46
Banks	40, 41
Baron of Baltimore	10
Behavior	31, 35
Belief	15, 16
Benefit of certain English statues secured to the people	10
Annapolis to have its	17
Bills	32, 33, 38, 40
Blood	14
Bonds of office to be sued by order of House of Delegates	36
of Sheriffs	52
of Comptroller and Treasurer	60
of State to be signed by Comptroller and Treasurer	61
of Lottery Commissioner	65
Books	37, 61, 69, 71
Borrowing	35, 40
Branches of Legislature	28, 66
Bribery	19, 20, 38
Buildings	45
Burthen	11
Burying ground	16
Business	31, 54
Calvert, Cecilius	10
Canals	62
Cancelling	61
Candidate, bribery in regard to	19
for office of Sheriff	53
new election, in case of tie	57, 66, 72
Cases of State in Court of Appeals, &c	59
criminal, Jury to be judges of law and fact	72
Census	28, 70, 73
Certificate	53, 61, 63
Certifying	38, 56, 58, 63
Challenge	38
Chancery	45, 53, 54, 55
Change of Constitution	17
of Residence	18
Charges not to be levied without consent of Legislature	11

INDEX.

	PAGE
Charges, criminal, copy of, to be furnished	13
of Clerks, &c., to be regulated	39
Charles the First	10
Charter of the State	10
of the City of Annapolis	17
of Banks	40
Chattels	16
Choosing	22, 59
Christians	16
Church	16
Circuit Courts	41, 44, 45, 46, 49, 50, 52, 53
Cities	53
Citizen	11, 18

City of Annapolis—see *Annapolis City*.
City of Baltimore—see *Baltimore City*.

City Council	52, 68
Civil cases, jurisdiction of, in Baltimore City	46, 47
removal of	56
Claims	46
Classification	29, 30
Clerks, their charges to be regulated	39
of Court of Appeals	42, 59
powers and duties of	49, 50
election of	54, 57
election returns to be made by	56, 58
Code	32, 33
Codification	32
Collectors	38
Colored population	13
Command in Chief	24
Commerce	17
Commissions, public	44
or fees not to be received by Judges, Comptroller, Treasurer, &c.	46, 59
to be issued to Sheriffs, Judges, &c., by Governor	52, 56, 64
of State's Attorneys to be prescribed	58
Commissioners to revise laws	32
to revise rules of practice	33
of county	51, 66, 67
of Public Works	62, 63, 64
of Lotteries	64, 65
of Land Office	65, 66
Commitment	36
Committee of the whole	31
Common Law	9
Common Pleas, Court for Baltimore City	46, 47, 48, 49, 50, 52
Community	12
Compact	9
Companies	34, 39, 70
Compensation of Governor	27
of Public Officers	35

INDEX. 87

Compensation of Senators and Delegates................................ 37
    of Clerks, Registers, &c.................................... 39
    for private property taken................................. 40
    of Judges of Court of Appeals.............................. 43
    of Judge of Circuit Court.................................. 46
    of Judges of Baltimore Courts.............................. 47
    of Judges of Orphans' Courts............................... 50
    of Justices of the Peace................................... 51
    of Chancellor, &c.. 54
    of State's Attorneys....................................... 58
    of Comptroller and Treasurer............................... 59
    of Commissioners of Public Works........................... 62
    of Lottery Commissioner.................................... 64
    of Commissioner of Land Office............................. 66
    of State Librarian... 66
    of Surveyors... 67
    of Wreck-master.. 68
    of Adjutant-General.. 70
    of officers generally...................................... 71
Competition... 62
Complaints.. 36
Comptroller of Treasury.......................26, 59, 60, 61, 65
Compulsion..13, 15, 31
Concurrence...39, 46
Conduct... 10
Congress.. 31
Congressmen... 18
Consanguinity..43, 53
Constables—see *Justices of the Peace.*
Construction.. 17
Contingent Fund... 33
Contracts..15, 34, 35, 65
Contribution..12, 15
Convention.........................9, 11, 24, 26, 30, 73
Conveyancing...33, 49
Conviction of criminals.................................14, 21
    of Public Officers....................39, 46, 48, 57, 58
Coroners.. 53
Corporations...34, 40
Corruption.. 14
Costs... 47
Counsel...13, 26, 53
Counties to be formed....................................... 68
County Commissioners..................................51, 66, 68
County seat of Baltimore County............................. 45
Courts, their use of English Statutes....................... 10
    Legislative, Executive and Judicial, powers to be separated....... 11
    evidence against oneself not to be compelled............... 13
    proceedings in, to be revised.............................. 33
    laws to be certified to.................................... 38
    the Judicial powers of the State........................... 41

INDEX.

Courts, the Circuit Courts..44, 45, 46
    Baltimore Courts...46, 47, 48
    Clerks..48, 49
    the Orphans' Courts, &c..50, 51
    trials by Jury... 72
Court House in Baltimore County.. 45
Court of Appeals..38, 41, 42, 43, 49, 50, 59
Courts Martial.. 25
Crime..12, 21, 35, 36
Criminal Court of Baltimore City..............................47, 48, 49, 50, 58
Cruelty... 12
Debate..11, 36
Debts not to be contracted by Legislature... 34
    of a husband... 38
    exemption from... 39
    imprisonment for... 40
Decisions of Governor to be reported to Legislature......................... 27
    of Court of Appeals to be published...................................... 42
Declaration of Rights... 9
Decrees in Chancery.. 54
Deeds.. 49
Defaulters... 38
Defence..13, 14, 35
Defendants... 55
Deficiencies.. 35
Delays..12, 13
Delegates, election district for... 18
    oath of office... 20
    returns of elections of Governor, &c...................................... 22
    apportionment of.. 28
    how elected—term of office... 29
    qualifications of... 30
    ineligibility of Congressmen.. 31
    disqualification to hold certain offices.................................. 35
    not liable for words in debate... 36
    provision for vacancies.. 36
    compensation... 37
    defaulting Collectors ineligible... 38
Delegation of Allegany Co... 70
Denial of justice... 12
Denominations of Religion..16, 17, 31
Departments of Government to be separate..................................... 11
    of power, rotation in.. 15
Devise... 16
Diminution of salaries, &c., forbidden...35, 43
Directors in Banks, liability of... 40
    in Rail Road and Canal Companies..................................... 62
Disfranchisement for perjury, &c... 37
Disqualification of Churches, Ministers, &c. from holding property....... 16
    for bribery, &c... 19
    of convicts, lunatics, &c... 21

INDEX. 89

	PAGE
Disqualification of Senators and Delegates	35, 36
of Judges, &c.	43, 53, 55
Distinction of departments of Government	11
Districts, provisions about removal	18
for election of Governor	23
for election of Judge of Court of Appeals	42
for Justices of the Peace	51
for election of Commissioners of Public Works	63
Divine Being	17
Divorce	34
Dockets	49
Duellists	38
Eastern Shore	23, 49
Elections to be free and frequent	10
qualifications of voters, &c.	18
bribery, illegal voting, &c.	19
disqualification of criminals	21
of Governor	22
of Senators and Delegates	28, 29, 31
provisions for vacancies	36
disqualifications	37
contested	41
of Judges of Court of Appeals	42, 43
of Judges of Circuit Courts	44, 45
of Baltimore Courts	46, 47
of Clerks of Courts	48
of Judges of Orphans' Courts and Registers of Wills	50
of Justices of the Peace and Constables	51
of Sheriffs	52
of Coroners, Elisors, Notaries, &c.	53
time of	54
provisions for death, &c., of Judges	55
returns of	56
cases of a tie, &c.	57
of State's Attorneys	58
of Treasurer, Comptroller, &c.	59
of Commissioners of Public Works	62, 63
of Lottery Commissioner	64
of Commissioner of Land Office	65
of State Librarian	66
of County Commissioners	66
of Road Supervisors and Surveyors	67
of Wreck-master	68
Sheriffs to give notice of	72
Elective Franchise	18
Electoral Districts	18, 19
Electors	19, 69
Eligibility of Governor	22
of Senators and Delegates	30, 31, 35
of Defaulters	38
of Clerks of Courts	48

INDEX.

	PAGE
Eligibility of Judges of Orphans' Courts, Registers of Wills, &c.	50
of Sheriffs, &c.	52, 53
of State's Attorneys.	57, 58
of Lottery Commissioner.	64
Elisor.	53
Enactments, style of laws.	32
passage of bills.	33
to carry into execution powers vested by the Constitution.	71
Endorsement.	60
England.	9, 10
Enumeration.	17
Equity.	10, 47, 49, 55
Establishment of Government.	9, 10
Evidences of witnesses, and against oneself.	13
Execution of laws not to be suspended.	11
of laws to be enforced by Governor.	24
exemption of property from.	39
of powers vested by the Constitution.	71
Executive powers of Government held in trust, &c.	10
to be distinct from Legislative and Judicial.	11
rotation of.	15
how elected, &c.	21
contingent fund.	33
appointments by.	35
Exemption.	35, 39
Exile.	13
Expenditure of public money.	33, 34
House of Delegates to inquire into.	36
for books, &c.	37
Comptroller, Treasurer, &c.	60
Expiration of term of office of Sheriff.	52
of offices of Chancellor, &c.	54
of Lottery Scheme.	65
Expulsion.	31, 36
Facts.	12, 72
Failure.	71
Faith.	34
Favor.	69, 73
Fees, not to be levied without consent of Legislature.	11
not to be received by Judges.	15, 43, 46
of Clerks, &c.	49, 50
of State's Attorney.	58
not to be received by Treasurer or Comptroller.	59
of Commissioner of Land Office.	66
over three thousand dollars to be paid to Treasurer.	71
Felony.	12, 35, 36
Fighting.	38
Fines may be imposed for the benefit of the community.	12
excessive not to be imposed.	13
for illegal voting.	19
may be remitted by Governor.	26

INDEX. 91
                       PAGE
Fines upon Directors and officers of Banks, &c........................... 40
Forces...19, 24
Foreign Powers 15
Forfeitures..14, 26, 41
Forms...9, 33, 60, 61
Foundation...9, 10
Franchise... 18
Freedom...10, 11, 12, 15, 55
Freeman..12, 13
Frequency... 11
Functions... 11
Fund...33, 61, 64, 65
General Assembly—see *Legislature.*
Gifts...16, 34
God..9, 15, 16, 17
Gospel...16, 31
Governor may remove Judges upon address of General Assembly...14, 43, 46
 oath of office... 20
 term of office... 21
 mode of election... 22
 Gubernatorial districts... 23
 qualifications... 23
 vacancies...23, 24
 his powers and duties.................................24, 25, 26, 27
 proclamation to convene Legislature............................... 30
 to issue warrants of election..................................... 37
 to sign bills.. 38
 to designate Chief Justice of Court of Appeals.................... 42
 to commission special Judges, in case of disqualification......... 43
 to sign public grants.. 44
 to appoint Justices of the Peace to fill vacancies................ 51
 to appoint Sheriffs, to fill vacancies, &c........................ 53
 to appoint Judges, to fill vacancies, &c.......................... 55
 returns of elections to be certified to........................56, 63
 to order new election in contested cases, &c..................57, 66
 to appoint Treasurer and Comptroller, to fill vacancies........... 59
 to appoint Adjutant-General...................................... 70
 to inspect returns of officers................................... 71
 to hold office until successor qualifies......................... 72
Government, origin, foundation, &c...................................... 9
 right of reform.. 10
 separation of departments.. 11
 seat of 11
 support of... 12
 militia, &c.. 14
 place of, may be changed... 26
 Governor to reside at seat of.................................... 27
 of police of Baltimore... 52
 laws to be passed to execute powers of........................... 71
Grand Inquest... 36
Grants under Charter of Charles the First............................... 10

92   INDEX.
                                                                   PAGE
Grants by the Legislature... 34
     of Lotteries prohibited.. 38
     of Charters for Banks, &c..................................... 40
     form of... 44
Gratitude to Almighty God.. 9
Great Seal... 38
Grievances... 11, 36
Guardianship.. 21
Guilt... 13
Happiness... 10
Honors.. 17
Houses of Assembly—see *Legislature*.
House of Delegates—see *Legislature*.
Husband and wife.. 38
Impartiality.. 13, 14
Impeachment... 11, 24, 26, 39
Imprisonment.. 13, 35, 40
Incompetency... 42, 43, 57
Independence.. 14
Indictment.. 13, 40, 44, 55, 56
Ineligibility—see *Eligibility*.
Information... 12, 26
Inhabitants... 9, 10, 68, 69
Injuries.. 12, 15
Injustice... 12
Inquest... 36
Inquiry... 36
Insolvent... 46
Inspection.. 61, 71
Institution.. 9
Insurrection.. 24
Integrity... 45
Interest.. 41, 43, 59, 62
Internal Improvements.................................... 34, 39, 61
Invasion.. 24
Jail.. 36
Jews.. 16
Journals.. 32, 62
Judges, separation of departments of Government................... 11
     independency of... 14
     oath of... 20
     each House of Legislature to be, in certain cases............. 31
     jurisdiction, Court of Appeals................................ 41
     opinions to be filed and published............................ 42
     Governor to designate Chief Justice........................... 42
     of Court of Appeals to appoint Clerk.......................... 42
     qualifications of, for Court of Appeals....................... 43
     term of office of, Court of Appeals........................... 43
     salary of, Court of Appeals................................... 43
     fees not allowed.. 43
     disqualification from affinity, &c............................ 43

INDEX. 93

	PAGE
Judges, to be conservators of the peace	44
qualifications of, for Circuit Courts	44, 45
jurisdiction of, Circuit Courts	45
term of office of, Circuit Courts	46
salary of, Circuit Courts	46
of Court of Common Pleas	46
its jurisdiction	46
of Superior Court of Baltimore City	46
its jurisdiction	46
qualifications of, for Baltimore Courts	47
salary of, Baltimore Courts	47
of Criminal Court of Baltimore City	47
its jurisdiction	47
salary, qualifications of Judges, &c	48
of Orphans' Courts	50
qualifications of, for Orphans' Courts	50
jurisdiction of, Orphans' Courts	50
compensation of, Orphans' Courts	50
vacancy in office of Register of Wills	51
appeals from Justice of the Peace	52
disqualification from affinity, &c	53
election of	54
vacancies	55
jurisdiction in Chancery cases	55
removal of cases	55
returns of elections of	56
cases of a tie, and contested elections	57
vacancy in office of State's Attorney	58
of Land Office	66
of rights of Jury in criminal cases	72
Judgment	13, 14
Jury	9, 13, 15, 40, 52, 72
Justice	12, 14
Justices of the Peace	31, 41, 46, 51, 52, 54
Knowledge to be encouraged	17
Land	16, 55
Land Office	65
Larceny	21
Laws of England, &c	9, 10
suspension of	11
preservation of	11
sanguinary	12
retrospective	12
of attainder	12
imprisonment of freemen	13
martial	14
holding two offices	15
oath of office	16
against illegal voting	19
to be enforced by Governor	24
recommendations of Governor	26

INDEX.

	PAGE
Laws, style of	32
mode of enactment	32
codification of	32
amendments of	32
passage of	33
statements about public money to be published with	34
when to take effect	37
to create office of Attorney-General not to be passed	37
to prohibit felons, &c., from voting	38
mode of attesting and recording	38
to protect wife's property	38
of exemption	39
to regulate Clerks' fees	39
about master and slave	40
granting Charters to Banks	40
to take private property for public use	40
about corporations	41
contested elections	41
about Justices of the Peace	51
about Coroners, &c	53
voters may practice	57
State's Attorneys' fees	58
Lease	16
Legislature, trustees of the public	10
right of the people to participate in	10
separation of departments of Government	11
alone to suspend laws	11
freedom of speech in	11
Annapolis to be the place of meeting	11
to be frequently convened	11
right of petition	11
taxes not to be levied, except by	11
to make laws about evidence	13
may make laws about free colored population	13
alone to raise standing armies	14
quartering soldiers	14
address of, to remove Judges	14
devises void, without leave of	16
duties of	17
to pass laws against illegal voting	19
oath of members of	20
provisions about election of Governor	22
to elect Governor, in case of death, &c	23
provisions about vacancies in recess	24, 25
Governor not to appoint persons rejected by	25
extra sessions of	26
recommendations from Governor	26
Governor to report to, reasons for pardons	26
to allow compensation to Counsel	27
to consist of two branches	28
election and classification of Senators	28, 29

INDEX.   95
                                                                PAGE
Legislature, apportionment of Delegates.............................. 28
      election of Delegates... 29
      time of meeting... 30
      time of adjournment... 30
      qualification of members.. 30
      persons ineligible.. 31
      powers of each House.. 31
      quorum.. 31
      sessions to be open... 31
      journals to be published.. 32
      special adjournments.. 32
      style of laws, and mode of enactment............................ 32
      commissioners for codification to be appointed.................. 32
      either House may originate bills................................ 33
      passage of bills.. 33
      appropriations of money to be made by law....................... 33
      contingent fund... 33
      statement of use of public moneys to be published............... 34
      divorces not to be granted...................................... 34
      debts not to be contracted...................................... 34
      credit of the State not to be granted........................... 34
      proceeds of internal improvement companies and State tax, to
        be used to pay public debt.................................... 34
      may borrow fifty thousand dollars............................... 35
      may contract debts for defence of the State..................... 35
      no extra compensation to be allowed............................. 35
      disqualification of members of.................................. 35
      each House may imprison... 35
      exemption from arrest... 35
      freedom of debate... 36
      House of Delegates may inquire into grievances, send for per-
        sons and papers, &c... 36
      vacancies... 36
      compensation.. 37
      books not to be purchased....................................... 37
      when laws to take effect.. 37
      may disfranchise certain persons................................ 37
      mode of attesting laws.. 38
      defaulting collectors and duelists ineligible 38
      Lotteries prohibited.. 38
      to pass laws about wife's property.............................. 38
      to pass exemption laws.. 39
      to adopt uniform rule for Clerks' charges....................... 39
      impeachments.. 39
      internal improvement companies.................................. 39
      not to abolish relation of master and slave..................... 40
      provision about Bank Charters................................... 40
      private property taken for public use to be paid for............ 40
      corporations to be formed under general laws.................... 41
      contested elections... 41
      usury... 41

INDEX.

Legislature, address of, to remove Judges..................43, 46
    to provide another Court.................................. 47
    to fix compensation of Judges of Orphans' Courts........... 50
    to fix number of Justices of Peace, their compensation, &c.... 51
    Coroners, Elisors and Notaries,............................ 53
    to provide for keeping Chancery Records................... 54
    contested elections for Judges, &c......................... 57
    reports of Comptroller.................................... 60
    reports of Commissioners of Public Works.................. 62
    to elect State Librarian.................................. 66
    provisions about County Commissioners..................... 66
    provisions about Road Supervisors......................... 67
    provisions about Surveyors................................ 67
    provisions about Wreck-master............................. 68
    New Counties... 69
    to pass laws about militia................................ 70
    to pass laws to carry out provisions of the Constitution... 71
    to regulate elections..................................... 72
    amendments to Constitution................................ 73
Liability..36, 40, 72
Liberty...9, 10, 12, 13, 14, 15, 17
Librarian... 66
Licenses.. 49
Literature.. 17
Lives...12, 13
Location..45, 69
Loss.. 61
Lot...22, 63
Lotteries...38, 65
Lunatics.. 21
Majority of each House to be a quorum..................... 31
    of each House required to pass bills...................... 33
    of House of Delegates to concur in impeachments........... 39
    of votes to call Convention............................... 73
Mankind... 10
Manufactures.. 17
Marines... 14
Maryland...9, 10, 68, 69
Master and Slave.. 40
Mayor of Baltimore.. 52
Means..9, 10
Meetings of Legislature to be frequent.................... 11
    of Legislature, extra..................................... 26
    of Legislature, regular................................... 30
    of Court of Appeals...................................... 42
Meeting-house... 16
Members of House of Delegates............................. 28
    of Senate.. 29
    of Legislature... 30
    of Legislature, persons ineligible....................31, 38
    of Legislature, exempt from arrest........................ 35

INDEX.   97
                                                            PAGE
Members of Legislature, compensation............................ 37
Members of Congress... 31
Mileage... 37
Military.....................................14, 15, 24, 25, 70, 72
Minister..15, 16, 31
Misbehavior, Judges removable for......................14, 43, 46
   Courts Martial... 25
   Clerk of Court of Appeals.................................. 42
   Clerks of Circuit Courts................................... 48
   Register of Wills.. 50
   State's Attorneys.. 57
Miscellaneous... 71
Money, penalties for giving, to procure votes................... 19
   not to be drawn from Treasury without appropriation........ 33
   publication of receipts and expenditures................... 34
   debts not to be contracted by Legislature.................. 34
   defaulting collectors ineligible........................... 38
   duties of Comptroller and Treasurer....................60, 61
   compensation of officers not to exceed three thousand dollars..... 71
   trial by Jury for all sums above five dollars.............. 72
Monopolies.. 17
Morality.. 15
Municipal Corporations.. 40
Name.. 20
Naval force... 24
Neglect..20, 43, 50
Negroes...13, 40
Newspaper... 26
Nobility.. 17
Nolle Prosequi.. 26
Nomination...24, 25
Non Compos.. 21
Non-resistance.. 10
Notaries.. 53
Notes... 40
Notice of application for pardon................................ 26
   of election for Senator or Delegate........................ 36
   of election of Commissioner of Land Office................. 66
Number of Senators and Delegates............................28, 30
   necessary to constitute quorum, &c......................... 31
   majority of votes necessary to pass laws................... 33
   majority of House to concur in impeachments................ 39
   two-thirds of each House to concur in address to remove Judges. 43
   of Justices of the Peace................................... 51
   of County Commissioners.................................... 67
   of population for New County............................... 69
   new election, when equal................................... 72
Oath, witnesses to be examined.................................. 13
   of office.. 16
   manner of administering.................................... 17
   form of.. 20

13

98   INDEX.

	PAGE
Oath, perjury	21
House of Delegates may inquire on	36
impeachments	39
to report of entries in book of receipts of officers	71
Offence	25, 35, 36
Officer, Judges not to hold any other office	14
no person to hold two offices	15
oath	16
disqualification of Ministers, &c	16
provisions about removals of voters	18
bribery	19
form of oath	20
perjury	21
military to be appointed by Governor	24
vacancies	25
persons rejected not to be appointed	25
time of nomination	25
term of office	25
removals	26
Senators' term of office	28
Delegates' term of office	29
qualification of Legislators	30
ineligibility	31
no extra compensation to be allowed	35
disqualifications of Legislators to hold certain offices	35
powers of Legislature to send for persons and papers	36
vacancies in office of Legislator	36
compensation of Senators and Delegates	37
disfranchisement for perjury, &c	38
defaulters ineligible	38
duelists ineligible	38
compensation of Clerks, &c., not to exceed twenty-five hundred dollars	39
of Banks not to borrow money	40
public commissioners	44
offices of Chancellor and Register abolished	54
returns of elections	56
new elections in cases of a tie, &c	57
qualifications of State's Attorneys	58
election, &c., of Comptroller and Treasurer	59
sundry officers	62
Commissioners of Public Works	62
Commissioner of Lotteries	64
Commissioner of Land Office	65
State Librarian	66
County Commissioners	66
Road Supervisors	67
Surveyors	67
Wreck-master	68
Militia	70
compensation of officers not to exceed three thousand dollars	71

INDEX. 99

	PAGE
Officer, continuation of certain persons in office	72
Opinion	42, 64
Oppression	10, 11, 12
Order	15
Origin	9, 33
Orphans' Courts	50, 55
Outlawry	13
Pains	12
Pardons	21, 26, 38
Partiality	20
Parsonage	16
Party, right of Jury trial	52
affinity to Judge	53
removal of cases	56
State cases in Court of Appeals, &c.	59
Paupers	11
Payment	19, 60, 61
Peace	14, 15, 44
Penalties, unusual not to be inflicted	12
for bribery	19
for perjury	21
for disorderly conduct	31
for non-attendance	31
against usury	41
People, State's Rights	9
right of reform	10
right of suffrage	10
trial of facts where they arise	12
independency of Judges	14
rights retained	17
elections	54
adoption of Constitution	73
amendments of Constitution	73
Perjury	21, 38
Perquisites	15, 43, 46, 58, 59
Persuasion	15, 16, 17
Petition	11, 27, 55
Place for meeting of Legislature	11
of trial of facts	12
search warrants	13
extra sessions of Legislature	26
of adjournment of Legislature	32
of meeting of Court of Appeals	42
of Offices of Treasurer and Comptroller	60
of holding elections	72
Plaintiff	46
Pleading	33
Plurality	22
Police	9, 52
Poll Tax	11
Population	28

100   INDEX.

	PAGE
Powers to alter or reform government	9
persons invested with, trustees of public	10
Legislative, Executive and Judicial to be separate	11
military	14
long continuance in, dangerous	15
executive vested in Governor	21
pardoning	26
of Governor to employ counsel	27
of each House of the Legislature	31
of House of Delegates	36
to disfranchise certain persons	37
judicial	41
of Circuit Judges	45
of Clerks, &c.	49
of Judges of Orphans' Court	50
of Commissioners of Public Works	62
of Treasurer in case of a tie	64
of County Commissioners	67
of Legislature to make laws to carry out Constitution	71
of Juries in Criminal Cases	72
Practice	10, 15, 33, 57, 58
Preacher	16, 31
Presents	15, 19
Presentment	56
President of Senate	24, 36
Press	17
Prince	15
Printing	38
Privileges	13, 17, 35, 37
Proclamation	30, 63
Profession	15, 17
Profits	15, 16, 20, 31, 35, 38
Prohibition	38
Promises	19
Property derived under Charter of the State	10
taxation	12
freemen not to be deprived of	13
search warrants	13
sales, &c. to Ministers, &c.	16
of wife to be protected	38
exemption laws	39
taken for public use	40
Prosecution	12, 36, 56
Protection	15, 38
Publication of Journals of Legislature	32
of statement about public moneys	34
of notice of election	36
of laws	38
of decisions of Court of Appeals	42
Publicity	31
Public Debt	34, 39, 61

INDEX. 101

PAGE

Public Works.. 62
Punishment, cruel and unusual, not to be inflicted..........12, 13
    ex post facto laws... 12
    criminal prosecutions...................................... 13
    of freemen.. 13
    witnesses and jurors belief in............................ 16
    for bribery... 19
    of disorderly members of Legislature...................... 31
    of other persons by Legislature........................... 35
    of bank officers.. 40
Purchase..37, 61
Qualifications for suffrage..........................11, 18, 21
    oath of office...16, 20
    of Governor..21, 22, 23
    of Senators and Delegates.............................30, 31
    of Judges of Court of Appeals.........................42, 43
    of Judges of Circuit Courts...........................44, 45
    of Judges of Baltimore Courts.........................47, 48
    of Clerks of Courts....................................... 48
    of Judges of Orphans' Courts.............................. 50
    of Register of Wills...................................... 50
    of Justices of the Peace.................................. 51
    of Sheriff..52, 53
    of Judges in cases of affinity, &c......................... 53
    in cases of a tie and contested elections................. 57
    of lawyers.. 57
    of State's Attorneys..................................57, 58
    of Comptroller and Treasurer..........................59, 60
    of sundry officers.. 62
Quartering.. 14
Questions... 32
Quorum.. 31
Rail Roads.. 62
Rate..41, 50, 62
Ratification.......................................54, 65, 69, 73
Reading of bills on three different days...................... 33
Reasons for pardons... 27
Recommendations of Governor...............................26, 27
Receipts..34, 60
Receivers...38, 58
Recess..24, 25
Records of Secretary of State................................. 27
    of Yeas and Nays.. 33
    House of Delegates may call for........................... 36
    of laws of the State...................................... 38
    Clerks to have custody of, &c.........................49, 50
    of Chancery Court... 54
    removal of cases.. 56
Redress...10, 11
Reference... 32
Reform...9, 10

102   INDEX.

	PAGE
Refusal...20, 24, 36, 37,	52
Regiments..	70
Registers, compensation...	39
election, &c..50, 51,	54
in Chancery 53,	54
cases of a tie, &c...	57
of land office...	66
Regulation of internal police of the State....................................	9
of the colored population..	13
about abolishing Chancery Court...............................	54
of jurisdiction in Chancery cases................................	55
for removal of cases..	55
of fiscal affairs by Comptroller.................................	60
Rejections...	25
Relations...43,	53
Religion...9, 15, 16,	17
Removal of Judges for misbehavior...	14
of voters..18,	19
of Governor from the State.......................................	24
of military officers..	25
of place of meeting of Legislature...............................	26
of Secretary of State..	27
of Senators and Delegates..	36
of Clerk of Court of Appeals.....................................	42
of Judges of Court of Appeals...................................	43
of Judges of Circuit Courts......................................	46
of Judges of Courts in Baltimore............................47,	48
of Clerks of Circuit Courts.......................................	48
of Register of Wills..50,	51
of Sheriffs...	52
of Judges, &c...	55
of cases..	56
of State's Attorneys..57,	58
of Surveyors..	68
of Wreck-masters...	68
Repeal..10, 32, 34,	41
Reports 32, 33, 42, 60,	61
Representation...28, 30, 69,	73
Reprieve..	26
Residence of voters...18,	19
of Governor...23,	27
of Senators and Delegates...................................30,	36
of Judges..43, 44,	45
of Sheriffs..52,	53
of Defendants in Chancery cases...............................	55
of State's Attorneys..	58
of sundry officers...	62
Resignation of officers elected..	21
of Governor, &c..23,	24
of Senators and Delegates..................................36,	37
of Judges, &c...	55

INDEX. 103

	PAGE
Resignation of Commissioners of Public Works	64
of Wreck-master	68
Returns of election for Governor	22
for Sheriff	53
for other officers	56, 57
for State's Attorneys	58
for Commissioners of Public Works	63
for Commissioner of Land Office	65, 66
to be regulated by Legislature	72
Revenue	36, 60
Rewards	16, 19, 46, 58
Rights	9, 10, 11, 12, 14, 15, 17, 72
Rivers	69
Roads	67
Rotation	15, 23
Rules	31, 33, 55
Safety	12, 15, 26
Salary—see *Compensation.*	
Sale	12, 16
Sciences	17
Seal	38, 44, 54
Search	13
Seat of Government	11, 26, 27, 60
Second	38
Secrecy	31
Secretary of State	22, 27
Sect	16
Security of liberty	9, 10
trial of facts where they arise	12
independence of Judges	14
bribery	19
of wife's property	38
Police of Baltimore City	52
to be given by sheriff	53
Seizure	13
Senate, oath of office	20
election of Governor	22
vacancy in office of Governor	24
consent of, to appointments by Governor	25, 27, 55, 59, 64 70
may be Convened alone	26
election of	28
classification	29
qualifications	30, 31
to keep Journal	32
special adjournment	32
disqualification	35
no liability for words in debate	36
compensation	37
ineligibility of defaulters and duelists	38
impeachment	39
consent of, to designation of Chief Justice	42

INDEX.

	PAGE
Sentence	25, 26
Separation	11, 69
Servant	35
Service	29, 35, 59, 64, 67
Sessions, election returns to, made to Legislature, at its commencement	22
extra, of Legislature	26
apportionment of members of House of Delegates	28
of Legislature, time of, determined	30
of Legislature to be open	31
of Legislature, special adjournment	32
bills to be read on three different days	33
statement about public monies to be published	34
exemption from arrest	35
per diem of Judges of Orphans' Court	50
Legislature to fix number of Justices of the Peace, &c	51
Chancery Court	53, 54
appointment of Treasurer, &c	59, 60
reports of Treasurer	61
reports of Commissioners of Public Works	62
sense of the people, about calling a convention to amend Constitution	73
Sheriffs	52, 66, 72
Sinking Fund	34
Slave	13, 40
Soldiers	14
Speaker of House of Delegates	22, 24, 36
Speech	11
State rights	9
charter	10
taxes	12
holding offices	15
disturbing the peace	15
titles of Nobility	17
Executive power of	21
divided into three Gubernatorial Districts	23
recommendations of Governor	26
reforms in legal proceedings, &c	33
appropriations of money	33
credit of, not to be loaned	34
extra compensation not to be allowed	35
jurisdiction of Courts, &c	45, 46
elections	54, 57
removal of cases	56
cases in Court of Appeals, &c	59
fiscal affairs of	60, 61
Public Works	62, 63
Statements	34, 36, 60, 61
State's Attorney—see Attorneys.	
State Librarian	66
State Treasurer	59, 64, 71
Statutes	10

INDEX. 105

	PAGE
Stocks	39, 60, 62
Stockholders	40, 62
Style of Legislature	28
of Laws	32
of Commissions, Writs, Indictments, &c	44
of Courts	45, 46, 47
of Commissioners of Public Works	62
Subordination	14
Subscription	37
Succession	16, 23
Successor of Justices of the Peace	51
of State's Attorneys	57, 58
of Comptroller and Treasurer	59, 60
of Lottery Commissioner	64
of State Librarian	66
of officers in Howard County	69
of Governor and other officers	72
Suffrage	10, 11, 18
Suggestion	56
Suit	36, 46, 55, 56, 71
Sum	33, 47, 66, 71
Superintendent	60, 62
Superior Court	46, 47, 48, 49, 50
Supervisors of Road	67
Support	11, 12, 16, 60
Surveyors	67, 68
Suspension	11, 25
Swearing	21
System	39, 65
Taxes	11, 12, 34, 60
Teacher	16
Tenure	14, 67, 72
Term of Governor	21
of officers appointed by Governor	25
of Secretary of State	27
of Senators	28
of Delegates	29
of Court of Appeals	42
of Judges of Court of Appeals	43
of Circuit Court	45
of Judges of Baltimore Courts	47
of Clerks of Baltimore Courts	48
of Registers of Wills	50
of Justices of the Peace	51
of Judges, &c	55
of Comptroller and Treasurer	59
of Commissioners of Public Works	63
of Lottery Commissioner	64
of Commissioner of Land Office	65
of State Librarian	66
of County Commissioners	66

106 INDEX.

	PAGE
Term of Road Supervisors	67
of Surveyors	67
of Wreck-master	68
of Adjutant General	70
of civil officers	72
Test	16
Ticket	66
Tie in election of Governor	22
in election of Senators and Delegates	36
in election of State's Attorney	58
in votes of Commissioners of Public Works	64
in election of Commissioner of Land Office	66
new election, provided for	72
Time of altering Constitution	9, 73
when English Statutes, &c., are applicable	10
allowed criminals for defence	13
of election of Governor	21
of qualification of Governor	22
of election of Governor in case of vacancy	23
of nomination of officers by Governor	25
of apportionment of Members of House of Delegates	28
of election of Delegates	29
of meetings of Legislature	30
of adjournment of Legislature	30
of special adjournments of Legislature	32
limited for passage of bills, &c.	33
for payment of debts of the State	34
when laws take effect	37
of meeting of Court of Appeals	42
of election of Judges of Orphans' Court	50
of election of Judges, Clerks, &c.	54
of abolishing Lotteries	65
of elections	72
Titles	17, 32
Tolls	62
Transfer	39, 60, 61
Treason	12, 35
Treasurer	26, 59, 60, 61, 64, 65, 71
Treasury	33, 35, 38
Trials by Jury	9, 13, 52, 72
of facts where they arise	12
disqualification of Judges, &c.	53
removals of	56
Trust	15, 16, 31, 38
Trustees	10
Unanimity	13
Uniformity	39
United States	15, 18, 23, 30, 31, 45, 73
Uprightness	14
Uses	10, 17, 34, 54
Usury	41

INDEX. 107
PAGE
Vacancy, in office of Governor... 24
 Governor to appoint in recess of Legislature..................... 25
 in office of Senator or Delegate...........................36, 37
 in office of Clerks.. 48
 in office of Register of Wills.................................... 51
 in office of Justice of the Peace................................. 51
 in office of Sheriff.. 52
 in office of Judge of Orphans' Court.............................. 55
 in office of State's Attorney..................................... 58
 in Treasury Department.. 59
 in office of Commissioner of Public Works......................... 64
 in office of Surveyor... 68
 in office of Wreck-master... 68
 on account of failure to pay over monies.......................... 71
Vested Rights.. 72
Virginia... 69
Virtue... 17
Viva Voce.. 22
Volunteers... 70
Voting, elective franchise determined.................................. 18
 bribery prohibited.. 19
 illegal, to be punished..19, 20
 oath in regard to... 20
 disqualifications... 21
 for Governor.. 22
 for Senators.. 28
 for Delegates... 29
 ineligibility... 31
 Yeas and Nays... 32
 to fill vacancies... 37
 for Judges of Circuit Courts...................................44, 47
 for Clerks.. 48
 for Judges of Orphans' Court...................................... 50
 for Register of Wills... 50
 for Justices of the Peace... 51
 for Sheriffs...52, 53
 for officers under New Constitution............................... 54
 election returns..56, 72
 in cases of a tie, &c...57, 72
 for State's Attorneys... 57
 for Comptroller and Treasurer..................................... 59
 for Commisssioners of Public Works................................ 62
 for Lottery Commissioner.. 64
 for Commissioner of Land Office................................... 65
 for State Librarian... 66
 for County Commissioners.. 66
 for Road Supervisors.. 67
 for Surveyor.. 67
 for Wreck-master.. 68
 for new county.. 69
 for adoption of Constitution...................................... 73

	PAGE
Wants	51
Wards	18, 19, 51
Warrants	13, 36, 37, 60, 61
Wars	14
Western Shore	49
Wife	38
Wills	39
Witnesses	13, 15, 36
Words	36
Worship	15, 16
Worth	12
Wreck-master	68
Writs	44, 66
Yeas—see *Ayes*.	

THE following lists of ACTS OF THE LEGISLATURE and DECISIONS OF THE COURT OF APPEALS are added for convenience of reference:

1852—ch. 12, 16, 17, 18, 20, 31, 34, 46, 48, 50, 51, 55, 56, 59, 62, 65, 68, 73, 74, 75, 76, 82, 86, 95, 111, 113, 122, 123, 136, 139, 154, 159, 169, 172, 173, 180, 183, 198, 214, 215, 219, 227, 231, 239, 247, 251, 263, 274, 290, 308, 312, 315, 323, 336, 341, 344, 351, 361. Res. 14.

1853—ch. 33, 36, 81, 82, 86, 102, 122, 123, 131, 133, 134, 147, 173, 181, 198, 201, 220, 238, 239, 242, 243, 244, 245, 271, 280, 299, 300, 320, 333, 335, 343, 372, 385, 391, 403, 406, 409, 415, 425, 441, 444, 448, 451.

1854—ch. 16, 18, 19, 26, 81, 135, 149, 152, 183, 196, 225, 236, 302, 325. Res. 5.

1 Md. 139, 368.— 2 Md. 62, 274, 341, 429.— 3 Md. 119.— 4 Md. 189.— 5 Md. 337, 370, 423.— 6 Md. 449, 468.

MURPHY & CO'S RECENT PUBLICATIONS.

☞ Any of the following Books will be sent by mail, prepaid, on receipt of the price annexed.

Just published, in 1 vol. 8vo. cloth, $1; law sheep, $1 50, law sheep, interleaved, $2.

The New Constitution of the State of Maryland, Reported and Adopted by the Convention of Delegates, assembled at the City of Annapolis, November 4, 1850, and Submitted to and Ratified by the People on the First Wednesday of June, 1851. With *Marginal Notes,* and References to Acts of the General Assembly and Decisions of the Court of Appeals, and an Appendix and Index.

By EDWARD OTIS HINKLEY, Esq., *of the Baltimore Bar.*

The Revenue Laws of Maryland. Published by order of the Legislature..8vo. law sheep $2

A NEW HISTORY OF MARYLAND.

Just published, in 1 vol. 12mo. Price $1.

The Day-Star of American Freedom; or the Birth and Early Growth of Toleration in the Province of Maryland. With a Sketch of the Colonization upon the Chesapeake and its tributaries, preceding the removal of the Government from St. Mary's to Annapolis; and a glimpse of the numbers and general state of society, of the religion, and legislation; of the life and manners of the men who worshipped in the wilderness at the First Rude Altar of Liberty.

By GEO. L.L. DAVIS, *of the Bar of Baltimore.*

McSHERRY'S HISTORY OF MARYLAND.

Recently published in 1 vol. 12mo. full cloth, library style $1.
School Edition, half Arabesque 75 cts.

A History of Maryland, from its settlement in 1634 to the year 1848, with an account of its first discovery, and the various explorations of the Chesapeake Bay, anterior to its settlement; to which is added, a copious APPENDIX, containing the names of the officers of the Old Maryland Line; the Lords Proprietary of the Province, and the Governors of Maryland, from its settlement to the present time, chronologically arranged; the Senators of the State, in the Senate of the United States; together with tables of the population of the counties, at each census, of the whole State, from its foundation; and questions on the principal events in the History, arranged according to Page and Chapter.

By JAMES MCSHERRY, Esq., *of the Frederick Bar.*

The *National Intelligencer* says:—"No State in the Union better deserves the labors of the historian, whether we regard her early settlement, her liberal charter, or the part she bore in the great revolution which made us a nation, or the number of eminent men born within her limits; and there is scarcely one of the original thirteen about which so little trouble has been taken to collect authentic notices The author's style is modest and unpretending, and the narrative is unexceptionable in sentiment We would invite the attention of our public schools to this book, as one well deserving to be introduced into such of the schools as embrace instruction in history."

BOZMAN'S HISTORY OF MARYLAND.

In 1 vol. of 1042 pages, royal 8vo. Library style, reduced in price from $5 to $3.

A History of Maryland, published by order of the State Legislature. The history of Maryland, from its settlement in 1633, to the restoration in 1660, with a copious introduction, and notes and illustrations. By JOHN LEEDS BOZMAN, Esq. In this work will be found a complete account of every event that occurred in the settlement and the succeeding thirty years, being the most interesting portion of the history of the State.

Just published, in 1 vol. 8vo. embossed cloth $1 50.

A History and Description of the Baltimore and Ohio Rail Road; With an Appendix, containing a full account of the ceremonies and procession attending the laying of the corner-stone, by Charles Carroll, of Carrollton, on the Fourth of July, 1828, and an original and complete report of the great opening celebration at Wheeling, January, 1853; to which is added a supplement. Illustrated by a Map and Six original Portraits. By a CITIZEN OF BALTIMORE.

In 2 vols. 8vo. cloth $5.

Maryland Medical and Surgical Journal, and Official Organ of the Medical Department of the Army and Navy of the United States.

MURPHY & CO'S RECENT PUBLICATIONS.

Recently published, in 1 volume, 4to., with Maps and Plates, $3 50.

Lynch's Exploring Expedition.—Official Report of the United States Exploring Expedition, to Explore the DEAD SEA and the River Jordan. By Lieut. W. F. LYNCH, U. S. N.

Recently published, in an 8vo. volume of 600 pages, neatly bound in embossed cloth, $2 50; cloth, gilt edges and sides, $3.

The Writings of DR. JOHN LOFLAND, the MILFORD BARD, with a Portrait of the Author and a Sketch of his Life. Collected and arranged by J. N. M'JILTON, A. M.

In 1 vol. 4to., Illustrated with Plates, Price $2 50.

Hall's Designs for Dwelling Houses, comprising a Series of Select, Original, and Modern Designs adapted to the Style of Building in the United States; with 24 Designs. For the use of Carpenters and Builders.

STANDARD GIFT BOOKS, SUITABLE FOR ALL SEASONS.

NEW, ENLARGED, UNIFORM AND BEAUTIFUL EDITIONS OF

BURNAP'S POPULAR LECTURES.

In 2 vols. 12mo., neatly bound in embossed cloth, $2; cloth, gilt edges and sides, $3. Either Volume will be sold separately.

The Sphere and Duties of Woman; a Course of Lectures; by George W. Burnap, LL. D. Illustrated with a fine Engraving.

Lectures to Young Men, on the Cultivation of the Mind, the Formation of Character, and the Conduct of Life; by George W. Burnap, LL. D. Illustrated with a Portrait of the Author.

The Publishers, in calling public attention to these valuable works, deem it unnecessary to add anything in the way of commendation. The high estimation in which Mr. Burnap's writings are held in this country and in Europe, are the best evidence of their general utility. These works have passed through several large editions in this country, and have been republished in England, where several large editions were sold immediately. They are now ranked as "STANDARD LITERATURE," and are, according to the statement of the English Press, "Destined to become Household Books."

AS USEFUL GIFT BOOKS, all Parents should place copies of these Works in the hands of their Sons and Daughters, and every Husband should give a copy to his Wife. The Lecture on the PRESERVATION OF HEALTH alone will amply repay them for the expenditure.

Just published, Fourth Edition, 8vo. cloth $2; library style $2 50.

BALMES' GREAT WORK ON CIVILIZATION!—*Protestantism and Catholicity Compared* in their Effects on the Civilization of Europe.

The Publishers have the pleasure to announce that near three thousand copies of this Great Work were sold in the first twelve months. It has been noticed in the most favorable terms by the press throughout the country. Every one who takes an interest in the subject ought to have a copy of this GREAT WORK of the AGE, that he might read it himself and lend it to his neighbor.

Recently published, in 5 vols. 8vo. cloth $10; library style, marbled edges, $12.

Bishop England's Works, published under the auspices and immediate superintendence of the late Rt. Rev. Bishop Reynolds, of Charleston.

The subjects of these volumes present attractions, not only to the inquirer after religious truth; but to the Statesman and the Lawyer they present much that is worthy of their study, as well for the subject matter, as for the style of the writer, and the simplicity of the language which he used to embody the analytical deductions made by his gigantic mind. His Discourses furnish Models of Oratory worthy of imitation by Divines, Statesmen, and members of the Legal Profession. It is difficult to say in what Dr. England excelled;—as an orator, he was great, sublime, thrilling;—as a Theologian, his profound erudition, and familiarity with the writings of the Fathers of the Church, and with Ecclesiastical History of all ages, and all countries, place him high amongst the highest:—as a Controversialist, the evenness of his temper, the lucidity of his reasoning, and the force of his language, command for him the respect of his antagonist, and the admiration of all his readers.

"We trust that Protestant and Catholic will vie with each other in shewing that they love literature and appreciate worth, without regard to sectarian prejudice." *Charleston Courier.*

"They deserve to take their place as contributions to American literature on the shelves of our libraries, and to find readers beyond the pale of the religious belief of their writer." *N. Y. Literary World.*

Just published, in 1 volume, 12mo. cloth, 75 cts.

The Studies and Teaching of the Society of Jesus, at the time of its suppression, 1750—1775. Translated from the French of M. L'ABBE MAYNARD, Honorary Canon of Poitiers, Professor of Rhetoric at Pontleroy.

This is a Historical Work, and unveils the *real secret of so much enmity to the Jesuits.*

MURPHY & CO'S RECENT PUBLICATIONS.

THE PEOPLE'S EDITION OF LINGARD'S ENGLAND.
Just published in 1 vol. 8vo., cloth $2; library style $2 50.

Lingard's History of England, abridged, with a continuation from 1688 to 1854.—By JAMES BURKE, Esq., Barrister at Law. With a Memoir of Dr. Lingard, and Marginal Notes, by M. J. KERNEY, A. M. Second Edition. Embellished with a fine steel Portrait of Dr. Lingard.

This highly important work is comprised in a beautiful octavo volume of nearly 700 pages; it is printed and bound in the best manner, and may justly be considered one of the cheapest books published.

We believe that it will be at once conceded, that at no period has it been of more importance than at the present to place before the American public a true and impartial history of England. No apology need therefore be made for the publication of an abridgment of Dr. Lingard's History of England, *at a price that will at once place it within the reach of all classes.*

A School Edition of this work has been published in 1 vol. 12mo. price $1.

LIBRARY EDITIONS OF FREDET'S UNIVERSAL HISTORIES.
In 2 volumes 12mo., cloth $2 50; library style, marbled edges, $3.
Either volume will be sold separately.

Ancient History, from the Dispersion of the Sons of Noe, to the Battle of Actium, and change of the Roman Republic into an Empire. By PETER FREDET, D. D., Professor of History in St. Mary's College, Baltimore. Fifth edition, carefully revised and enlarged.

Modern History, from the Coming of Christ and the change of the Roman Republic into an Empire, to the year of our Lord 1854. By PETER FREDET, D. D., Prof. of History in St. Mary's College, Baltimore. Eleventh enlarged and improved edition.

These two volumes form a complete connection or continuous chain of historical events from the creation of the world to the year 1854.

Recently published, in 1 volume, 12mo. 75 cents.

Willitoft, or the Days of James the First. A Tale. By JAS. MCSHERRY, Esq., author of *McSherry's History of Maryland.*

Recently published, in a neat 32mo. volume, Embellished with a Map of the City and Views of the Principal Public Buildings. Price 25 cents.

The Stranger's Guide in Baltimore, showing the easiest and best mode of seeing all the Public Buildings and places of note in and around the City, and in the neighborhood; together with some brief observations on its Trade, Resources, Prosperity, Commercial Advantages and Future Prospects. By a BALTIMOREAN.

Second Enlarged Edition, in a neat 32mo. vol., fancy paper, gilt 25 cents; cloth 38 cents; cloth, gilt edges, 50 cents.

Etiquette at Washington, together with the Customs adopted by Polite Society in the United States. To which is added an Appendix, containing a Description of the Public Buildings, and some of the Principal Objects of interest to a Stranger visiting Washington.

The public favor with which this little work has been received, and the rapidity with which the first edition sold, has induced the Publishers to enlarge and improve the present to nearly double the size of the former edition.

American Etiquette, being a complete guide for Ladies and Gentlemen, in their intercourse with society, containing the most complete modes and customs in use in the United States..................32mo. cloth, 25....cloth, gilt edges, 38

The Present Political Condition and Prospects of Spain. A Lecture delivered before the Maryland Institute for the Promotion of the Mechanic Arts, by S. TEACKLE WALLIS, Esq.,...paper 13

Washington's Farewell Address to the People of the United States, September, 1796. Embellished with a neat and appropriate Border. Printed in three colors, on a sheet 20x24 inches, suitable for Framing. Price 12½ cents.

A copy of this Address ought to have a conspicuous place in every School-room in the United States, as well as in the Counting-room and Office of every lover of the Father of his Country.

Washington, the Model of Character for American Youth....paper 13

Pope's Essay on Man......................................32mo. cloth 13

THE AMUSING LIBRARY,

A New Series of ORIGINAL TALES, TRANSLATIONS AND REPRINTS OF POPULAR WORKS.

Neat, Cheap, and Attractive Volumes for Home, Railway or Steamboat Travelling; Also, for Presents, Premiums, &c.

The object contemplated by THE AMUSING LIBRARY is to provide a choice supply of Books of Light Reading, entirely free from objectionable matter, and which may be indiscriminately used by young and old. In the selection, great pains will be taken to admit no Work that is not in every respect adapted for the perusal of all who desire a *sound* and *healthy imaginative literature, free from every thing immoral* on the one hand, or *controversial* on the other. The volumes while issued at a price which bring them within the reach of all, yet possess sufficient attractions of typography and embellishment to fit them for the drawing-room table and for presents.

It is proposed to comprise a choice selection of the best of the imaginative writings of various countries. With original tales and reprints of home authors will be united the best fictions of other lands,—Belgian, French, German, Spanish, Italian, &c.; and as the scenes will be laid in different countries and at different periods, the volumes will not only furnish amusing reading, but will likewise convey, especially to the youthful reader, much historical and other information.

In pursuance of this idea, the Editors have much gratification in announcing that they have made an arrangement with the distinguished Belgian Novelist, M. Henri Conscience, by which they will be enabled to include in their Library an authorized edition of all his works. They are also in communication with several other foreign authors of distinction, whose works will be speedily announced.

Just published in a neat vol. demi 8vo.; price in Extra Cloth, gilt backs, 75 cents; in Cloth, gilt edges and sides, $1.

THE CURSE OF THE VILLAGE, and THE HAPPINESS OF BEING RICH.

Two Tales in one volume, Embellished with a very neat Frontispiece.

From the Original Flemish of HENDRIK CONSCIENCE.

The *London Athenæum* in noticing this volume, says:—'These two tales by the favorite popular novelist of Belgium will do his reputation no dis-service. The first may be called a temperance story, such as would delight the heart of Mr. Gough or Mr. Cruikshank."

The *London Weekly Times* says:—"The first of these tales is a vigorous description of the evils of drunkenness, and the whole story is touching in the extreme."

Just Published, uniform with the above,

THE LION OF FLANDERS; or, The Battle of the Golden Spurs.

A Historical Romance of the Glorious Days of Flanders.

The *Revue des deux Mondes*, says:—"This romance displays a talent full of vigor and skill. The picture, especially, with which it closes, is a masterpiece of art and power."

The *Church of England Quarterly*, says:—"*The Lion of Flanders* at once stamped its writer as a man of mark. Having once taken up a volume of this stirring narrative, we found the greatest difficulty in laying it down; indeed, since the publication of the Waverly Novels, we have never been so absorbed by any work of fiction."

Just published, uniform with the above,

VEVA; OR, THE WAR OF THE PEASANTS.

A Historical Tale of the Eighteenth Century. With a Frontispiece and Vignette.

This beautiful tale preserves the memory of the grand though unavailing struggle of the Flemings to uphold their religion and liberties against the armies of the French Republic, and thus ranks with those narratives which recount the immortal deeds of the Vendeans and the Chouans. The Author throws himself amidst the events he relates with characteristic impetuosity, and has lavished on the story all the power and grace of his vivid and picturesque style. It is in part a love-story, and more of a historical romance, in the English sense of the word, than most of the author's works; yet it is nevertheless scrupulously accurate in statement, and never in any way violates historical truth.

The *Hastings News* says:—"The 'War of the Peasants' portrays the inimitable self-devotion of the patriots who sought vainly to stay the march of French armies into Belgium. It is a book that stirs our feelings and warms our blood; but the emotions it awakens are generous, and the fire enkindled is that holy fire of patriotism, which God forbid should ever become extinct in any land."

The *Soirées Bruxelloises* says:—"Whatever may be the value of the romances published this year, there is not one of them which comes near the 'War of the Peasants' of M. Hendrik Conscience. Every where the reader is under the influence of a powerful fascination, and his interest is most vividly excited."

NEARLY READY, uniform with the above,

TALES OF OLD FLANDERS: Count Hugo of Craenhove; Wooden Clara.

The *Revue des Deux Mondes* says:—"Nothing can be more admirable than the picture which this legend of Old Flanders presents. The poetry of its details, the delicacy of its sentiments, and the melancholy grace which pervades it, lend it a charm which is irresistible."

THE MISER; RICKETICKETACK.

"The success of Conscience's writings is a blessing and a boon. It is matter of congratulation that every one reads, and wishes to read again, these books so tender, so gentle, so simple, so familiar and touching, chosen friends and companions of every honest heart and of every cultivated mind. We have much to learn from him in concealed but most real art, in delicacy of touch, in genuineness of emotion, in native gracefulness, in the secret of that refined proportion and perspective which talent alone cannot teach,—which may be manifested in thirty pages, and which one may strive after in vain through a hundred volumes." *M. de Pontmartin* ("Causeries Littérairs.")

MURPHY & CO., PUBLISHERS, &c., 178 Market Street, Baltimore.

Printed in Poland
by Amazon Fulfillment
Poland Sp. z o.o., Wrocław

68552978R00074